Nickel-Cobalt Laterites—A Deposit Model

By Erin Marsh, Eric Anderson, and Floyd Gray

Chapter H of
Mineral Deposit Models for Resource Assessment

Scientific Investigations Report 2010–5070-H

U.S. Department of the Interior
U.S. Geological Survey

U.S. Department of the Interior
SALLY JEWELL, Secretary

U.S. Geological Survey
Suzette M. Kimball, Acting Director

U.S. Geological Survey, Reston, Virginia: 2013

For more information on the USGS—the Federal source for science about the Earth, its natural and living resources, natural hazards, and the environment, visit http://www.usgs.gov or call 1–888–ASK–USGS.

For an overview of USGS information products, including maps, imagery, and publications,
visit http://www.usgs.gov/pubprod

To order this and other USGS information products, visit http://store.usgs.gov

Suggested citation:
Marsh, Erin, Anderson, Eric, and Gray, Floyd, 2013, Nickel-cobalt laterites—A deposit model, chap. H *of* Mineral deposit models for resource assessment: U.S. Geological Survey Scientific Investigations Report 2010–5070–H, 38 p., http://pubs.usgs.gov/sir/2010/5070/h/.

Contents

Figures

Tables

Conversion Factors

SI to Inch/Pound

Multiply	By	To obtain
Length		
meter (m)	3.281	foot (ft)
kilometer (km)	0.6214	mile (mi)
Area		
square kilometer (km^2)	0.3861	square mile (mi^2)
Mass		
megagram (Mg)	1.102	ton, short (2,000 lb)
megagram (Mg)	0.9842	ton, long (2,240 lb)
Density		
gram per cubic centimeter (g/cm^3)	62.4220	pound per cubic foot (lb/ft^3)

Abbreviations

Al	Aluminum
Ar	Argon
Au	Gold
Ca	Calcium
Co	Cobalt
CO_2	Carbon dioxide
Cu	Copper
Cr	Chromium
EM	Electromagnetic
Fe	Iron
FTIR	Diffuse reflectance infrared Fourier transform spectroscopy
GPR	Ground penetrating radar
He	Helium
HPAL	High-pressure acid leaching
IP	Induced polarization
K	Potassium
Ma	Million years ago (mega-annum)
Mg	Magnesium
Mn	Manganese
Nb	Niobium
Ni	Nickel
PGE	Platinum group element
Si	Silica
SX-EW	Solvent extraction–electrowinning
TDS	Total dissolved solids
Th	Thorium
Ti	Titanium
TSS	Total suspended solids
U	Uranium
wt%	Weight percent
Y	Yttrium
Zn	Zinc
Zr	Zirconium

Nickel-Cobalt Laterites—A Deposit Model

By Erin Marsh, Eric Anderson, and Floyd Gray

Abstract

Nickel-cobalt (Ni-Co) laterite deposits are supergene enrichments of Ni±Co that form from intense chemical and mechanical weathering of ultramafic parent rocks. These regolith deposits typically form within 26 degrees of the equator, although there are a few exceptions. They form in active continental margins and stable cratonic settings. It takes as little as one million years for a laterite profile to develop. Three subtypes of Ni-Co laterite deposits are classified according to the dominant Ni-bearing mineralogy, which include hydrous magnesium (Mg)-silicate, smectite, and oxide. These minerals form in weathering horizons that begin with the unweathered protolith at the base, saprolite next, a smectite transition zone only in profiles where drainage is very poor, followed by limonite, and then capped with ferricrete at the top. The saprolite contains Ni-rich hydrous Mg-silicates, the Ni-rich clays occur in the transition horizon, and Ni-rich goethite occurs in the limonite. Although these subtypes of deposits are the more widely used terms for classification of Ni-Co laterite deposits, most deposits have economic concentrations of Ni in more than one horizon. Because of their complex mineralogy and heterogeneous concentrations, mining of these metallurgically complex deposits can be challenging. Deposits range in size from 2.5 to about 400 million tonnes, with Ni and Co grades of 0.66–2.4 percent (median 1.3) and 0.01–0.15 percent (median 0.08), respectively. Modern techniques of ore delineation and mineralogical identification are being developed to aid in streamlining the Ni-Co laterite mining process, and low-temperature and low-pressure ore processing techniques are being tested that will treat the entire weathered profile. There is evidence that the production of Ni and Co from laterites is more energy intensive than that of sulfide ores, reflecting the environmental impact of producing a Ni-Co laterite deposit. Tailings may include high levels of magnesium, sulfate, and manganese and have the potential to be physically unstable.

Introduction

Nickel-cobalt (Ni-Co) laterites are supergene deposits of nickel (Ni) ± cobalt (Co) formed from the pervasive chemical and mechanical weathering of ultramafic rocks. The formation of secondary concentrations of Ni±Co substantial enough for an economic resource requires a protolith lithology that is primarily enriched in Ni. Ultramafic rocks can contain as much as 0.3 percent Ni (Lelong and others, 1976). These rocks occur within ophiolite complexes as harzburgite and dunite or within komatiites and layered complexes as peridotites and dunites (Brand and others, 1998). The extreme weathering breaks down all susceptible primary minerals. Their chemical components are dispersed in groundwater or become incorporated into altered or new minerals that are stable in the weathering environment. The residual material can average as much as 5 percent Ni and 0.06 percent Co (Freyssinet and others, 2005). Since Ni-Co laterites were first studied, scientists recognized that the enrichment of Ni in the weathering profile is controlled by several interplaying factors, as with the development of all pedoliths, that include parent rock, climate, chemistry/rates of chemical weathering, drainage, and tectonics (Norton, 1973; Lelong and others, 1976; de Vletter, 1978; Golightly, 1981, 2010; Ogura, 1986; Gleeson and others, 2003; Freyssinet and others, 2005).

The Ni-Co laterites have been classified on the basis of their weathering profile and their mineralogical characteristics. Wet, wet-to-dry, and dry-to-wet climate scenarios are used to classify Ni-Co laterites with regard to the weathering profile and the interplay of the factors mentioned above (Golightly, 1981, 2010). These three regional climate scenarios help describe the variation in Ni-Co laterite deposits (table 1). This classification focuses more on process than product, whereas the mineralogical characteristics classification relies on the products formed by these processes. This deposit model will concentrate on the mineralogical classification and illustrate that the factors involved in the development of the weathering profile are key to the concentration of Ni and Co in particular minerals. The mineralogical characteristics subdivide the Ni-bearing ores into oxide, clay, or hydrous magnesium (Mg)-silicate subtypes, which have critical differences in their profile development, structure, and chemistry that affect extraction and processing techniques (Samama, 1986; Brand and others, 1998; Gleeson and others, 2003; Freyssinet and others, 2005; Golightly, 2010). All three mineralogical types of ore may be present in a single Ni-Co laterite deposit. The metalliferous laterite deposits are mineralogically complex, discontinuous, and commonly have Ni enrichment in more than one of the weathering profile zones (Lelong and others, 1976). Some deposits are subsequently mechanically weathered, redeposited, reconcentrated, and possibly covered by new sediment (Golightly, 1981).

Table 1. Factors defining the climate scenarios used to describe the variation in nickel-cobalt laterite deposits (Golightly, 1981, 2010).

[Ni, Nickel; Co, Cobalt; Mg, Magnesium]

Climate scenario	Tectonic stablity	Terrane	Climate	Profile development
Wet	Active uplift	Elevated	Rainforest	Ni in hydrous Mg-silicates
Wet-to-dry	Stable peneplain	Flat	Increasing aridity/time	Ni and Co in the oxide, clay transition zone
Dry-to-wet	Dissected peneplain	Elevated	Increasing moisture/time	Ni and Co in clay and saprolite zones

The Ni-Co laterite deposits make up 72 percent of the global Ni resource and only 50 percent of the global Ni produced (M. Elias, Nickel at CSA Global Pty Ltd., written commun., 2012). This disparity stems from the expense and complexity of the metallurgy involved in extracting Ni from the mineralogically diverse and erratic Ni concentrations through a laterite profile. Three different processes are used to extract Ni and Co from the respective enriched layers. The processes include either the Caron process or high-pressure acid leaching (HPAL) for the oxide subtype ore, HPAL for clay subtype ore, and a smelting process for hydrous Mg-silicate subtype ore (Elias, 2002; Dalvi and others, 2004). Because of the current metallurgical intricacies encountered while dealing with heterogeneous Ni-Co laterite profiles, a number of recent studies have focused on ore delineation and mineralogical identification, including the application of diffuse reflectance spectroscopy to distinguish ore mineralogy (Basile and others, 2010; Wells and Chia, 2011). A new ore-processing technique, DNi, was developed by Direct Nickel to treat the entire laterite profile. This innovation is a hydrometallurgical process capable of extracting 95 percent of the Ni and 85 percent of the Co in laterites (Direct Nickel, 2010). With the potential success of the DNi hydrometallurgical process or any other low-temperature and low-pressure Ni-Co laterite processing, these supergene deposits will be a much larger contributor to the future production of Ni and Co.

The Ni-Co laterite deposits are an important source of Ni. Currently, there is a decline in Ni resources (Dalvi and others, 2004) in Ni-bearing magmatic sulfide lode deposits (for example, Schulz and others, 2010; Naldrett, 2011). New efforts to develop an alternative source of Ni, particularly with improved metallurgical processing, make the Ni-Co laterites an important exploration target in anticipation of the future demand for Ni. Although this model is defined as a Ni-Co laterite model, not every deposit classified by this model has a mining history with recovered Co. Although Co may not be recovered from every deposit, it commonly is present at economic levels. This deposit model provides a general description of the geology and mineralogy of Ni-Co laterite deposits and contains a discussion of the influences of climate, geomorphology (relief), drainage, tectonism, structure, and protolith on the development of favorable weathering profiles. This model of Ni-Co laterite deposits represents part of the effort of the U.S. Geological Survey Mineral Resources Program to update the existing models to be used for an upcoming national mineral-resource assessment.

Deposit Type and Associated Commodities

The Ni-Co laterites are regolith or supergene deposits of Ni±Co. They are the product of prolonged and pervasive mechanical and chemical weathering of harzburgite, dunite, and peridotites and their metamorphic derivatives, such as serpentinite. They can be associated with platinum group element (PGE) placers (Cox and Singer, 1986). The primary commodity is Ni; the most common associated commodity is Co. These deposits have a geochemical association with iron (Fe), Mg, and chromium (Cr) and, less consistently, with zinc (Zn), copper (Cu), and PGEs (Lelong and others, 1976; Derkmann and Jung, 1986; Alcock, 1988; Brand and others, 1998).

Other deposits genetically related to Ni-Co laterites are bauxites and gold (Au), Fe, niobium (Nb), and phosphate laterite deposits (Freyssinet and others, 2005). Magmatic Ni sulfide and podiform Cr deposits may be present in the same region as Ni-Co laterite deposits because of their association with various ultramafic intrusions.

Example Deposits

There are three major subtypes of Ni-Co laterite deposits—hydrous Mg-silicate, clay, and oxide. The Ni-Co laterites can occur surficially as in situ deposits, buried as karst (Albania and Greece), or as linear/fault-hosted deposits (Urals) (Golightly, 1981). This model will mainly focus on the in situ deposits.

Linear- and karst-type deposits share some mineralogical similarities to in situ deposits but have added complexities because of their setting in fault zones or along unconformities between ultramafic and carbonate rocks. They may have experienced more extensive secondary transport and enrichment than those that have been simply reconcentrated because of downslope erosion from plateaus to lowlands, as seen in Brazil and Cuba (for example, Glaskovsky and others, 1977; Maksimovic, 1978; Valeton and others, 1987; Eliopoulos and Economou-Eliopoulos, 2000; Freyssinet and others, 2005). The karst-type deposits may deserve a deposit model of their own. Not only are the deposits located on unconformity surfaces, but they also are commonly derived from mixtures of ultramafic and felsic parent material, so they can have bauxite attributes (Maksimovic, 1978; Laznicka, 1985). Additionally, they contain takovite, a Ni-bearing hydrated carbonate mineral that is not seen in other Ni-Co laterite deposits (Valeton and others, 1987; J.P. Golightly, Golightly Geoscience, written commun., 2012). The final enrichment of Ni varies from in situ deposits in that many of the karst-type deposits are noted to have been diagenetically altered or metamorphosed to pumpellyite through greenschist and possibly as high as amphibolite facies (Mposkos, 1981; Valeton and others, 1987; Economou-Eliopoulos, 2003; M. Economou-Eliopoulos, cited by J.P. Golightly, Golightly Geoscience, written commun., 2012), with a mineralogy of hematite, quartz, and nimite as the main Ni-bearing mineral (Zevgolis and others, 2010). Unlike the minerals that weather to form in situ Ni-Co laterite deposits, the precursors (chrysotile, clinochlore, talc, and perocaite) to the supergene enrichment of Ni in deposits in the Urals are products of low-grade metamorphism (Talovina and others, 2007; Dill, 2010).

It is helpful to look at specific occurrences to illustrate the development and diversity of Ni and Co in a laterite deposit. The Nickel Mountain deposit in Riddle, Oregon, is a hydrous Mg-silicate subtype Ni laterite, although for this type of deposit it has a relatively low average grade of 1.18 percent Ni. It is given as an example here because it is the only economically substantial deposit in the continental United States. The Ni-Co laterite deposits in New Caledonia, the Dominican Republic, Indonesia, and Guatemala, as well as minor occurrences in California and North Carolina, are also hydrous Mg-silicate subtype deposits (Ross and others, 1928; Troly and others, 1979; Foose, 1992). Murrin Murrin in Western Australia is a classic clay ore Ni-Co laterite deposit. The Cawse deposit in Western Australia is an oxide ore Ni-Co laterite deposit, as are many of the deposits in Cuba. The Goro deposit in New Caledonia contains minable Ni concentrations in the limonite (less than or equal to 1.7 percent Ni and 0.5 percent Co), smectite (less than or equal to 2 percent Ni and 0.5 percent Co), and saprolite (less than or equal to 3 percent Ni) layers of the laterite profile (Goro Nickel, 2008). More detailed grade and tonnage summaries of known Ni-Co laterite deposits are presented by Berger and others (2011). The details of the Nickel Mountain deposit, as well as the more well-known hydrous Mg-silicate, clay, and oxide subtype deposits from outside the United States, are summarized below.

Nickel Mountain, Riddle, Oregon

The Nickel Mountain deposit is in the Klamath Mountains near Riddle, Oregon. Its setting is unusual in that it lies farther than 26 degrees from the equator (fig. 1); most of the other Ni-Co laterite deposits are within 26 degrees. The Nickel Mountain deposit developed from the Tertiary weathering of Jurassic peridotite, dunite, and serpentinite. The orebodies are at the crest of the uplifted Klamath Peneplain and along the terrace below. The top of the laterite profile has been weathered away, leaving only the saprolite layer with a thin, oxide-weathered cap that developed during more recent exposure

(fig. 2; Chace and others, 1969). The average Ni grade was between 1.18 and 1.5 percent; a total of 26.7 million tonnes (Mt) was produced between 1954 and 1998, and an estimated total size of the deposit was 63.8 Mt (Cumberlidge and Chace, 1968; D.F. Briggs, unpub. data, 2006; Eckstrand and others, 2008; U.S. Geological Survey, 2011). Although hydrous Mg-silicate is the dominant ore at Nickel Mountain, 20 percent of the reserve is held in oxides (U.S. Geological Survey, 2011).

Falcondo District, Dominican Republic, Hispaniola

Mineral resources, inclusive of reserves, for the Falcondo property reported by Xstrata, on June 30, 2010, were 39.7 Mt grading at 1.55 percent Ni (measured), 34.5 Mt grading at 1.56 percent Ni (indicated), and 4.9 Mt grading at 1.4 percent Ni (inferred) (Xstrata, 2011). This district developed from the weathering of ultramafic rocks of the Loma Caribe ophiolite—serpentinized harzburgite with some dunite, lherzolite, and pyroxenite—of the northern margin of the Caribbean Plate that was emplaced during the late Albian (Lewis and others, 2006; Proenza and others, 2008). Uplift of this region took place in the late Oligocene followed by transpression due to movement along a regional strike-slip fault. This tectonic activity caused continual fluctuation in elevation, keeping the water table low and promoting development of a complete hydrous Mg-silicate subtype laterite profile with a well-developed saprolite horizon that contains most of the ore reserves and the highest grade of Ni (Lewis and others, 2006; Berger and others, 2011). Weathering began during the early Miocene (Lewis and other, 2006).

The laterite profile consists of unaltered serpentinized harzburgite at the base, then an overlying hard saprolite zone (40 percent of the reserves; 1.74 percent Ni) that transitions through a soft saprolite zone (31 percent of the reserves; 1.7 percent Ni) upward into a nickeliferous limonite zone (21 percent of the reserves; 1.42 percent Ni). It is capped by a thin layer of ferricrete or hematite cap (fig. 3; Berger and others, 2011). Nickel-bearing minerals include poorly crystalline hydrous Mg-silicates (approximately 10 angstrom and approximately 7 angstrom garnierites), serpentine, smectite, gibbsite, goethite, and falcondite (Berger and others, 2011; Villanova-de-Benavent and others, 2011). Ferguson and others (1979) commented that Co was found in the transition between the limonite and saprolite horizons in the weathered profile. Lewis and others (2006) mentioned the presence of asbolane at the base of the limonite zone and Co grades of as much as 0.25 weight percent (wt%); however, because smelting is used to process the ore, Co is not recovered.

Murrin Murrin, Western Australia

The Murrin Murrin deposit contained a resource of 268 Mt at 1.01 percent Ni and 0.074 percent Co, with reserves of 196 Mt at 1.05 percent Ni and 0.078 percent Co in 2010 (Minara Resources Limited, 2010). The topography of the area is generally low and subdued. The ore deposit developed from

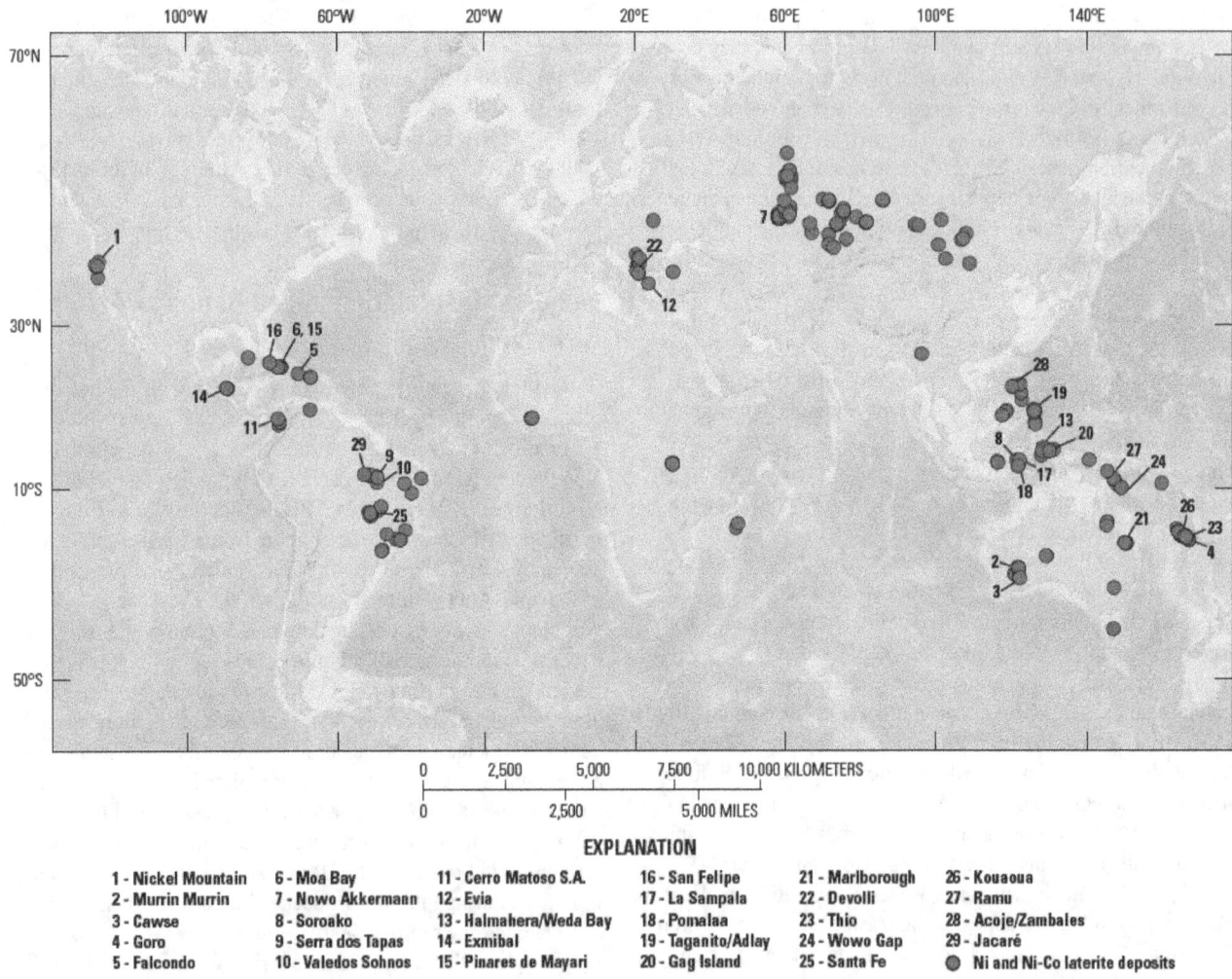

EXPLANATION

1 - Nickel Mountain	6 - Moa Bay	11 - Cerro Matoso S.A.	16 - San Felipe	21 - Marlborough	26 - Kouaoua
2 - Murrin Murrin	7 - Nowo Akkermann	12 - Evia	17 - La Sampala	22 - Devolli	27 - Ramu
3 - Cawse	8 - Soroako	13 - Halmahera/Weda Bay	18 - Pomalaa	23 - Thio	28 - Acoje/Zambales
4 - Goro	9 - Serra dos Tapas	14 - Exmibal	19 - Taganito/Adlay	24 - Wowo Gap	29 - Jacaré
5 - Falcondo	10 - Valedos Sohnos	15 - Pinares de Mayari	20 - Gag Island	25 - Santa Fe	● Ni and Ni-Co laterite deposits

Figure 1.   Global distribution of nickel (Ni) and nickel-cobalt (Ni-Co) laterite deposits. Locations from the Geological Survey of Canada World database of platinum group elements, nickel, and chromium deposits (Eckstrand and others, 2008) and U.S. Geological Survey Open-File Report 2011–1058 (Berger and others, 2011).

thoroughly serpentinized peridotite, which was a komatiitic olivine cumulate in the Late Archean Norseman-Wiluna green-stone belt (Monti and Fazakerley, 1996; Wells and Butt, 2006). The cumulate exhibits all textural variations from orthocumu-late to adcumulate (Gaudin and others, 2005). This important feature has an effect on the thickness and development of the weathered zones in the laterite profile. The serpentinized peridotite contains 0.2 percent Ni, mostly hosted in lizardite (Gaudin and others, 2005). Two areas of serpentinized perido-tite outcrop in the Murrin Murrin area.

The laterite profile consists of five main horizons upward, which include unweathered serpentinized peridotite at the base, saprolite, smectite, limonite (known as the ferruginous zone at Murrin Murrin), and a cap of duricrust and unconsoli-dated sediment (fig. 4). Intercalated with these main weather-ing horizons are minor mineral horizons of Fe-rich saprolite, which can occur at the top of the saprolite in the transition to the smectite zone; an Fe-rich smectite zone at the transition to the limonite; manganese (Mn)-oxide pods and lenses enriched in Co and Ni; silicate- and magnesite-rich veins and fracture fill; and pods and layers of kaolinite and chlorite plastic clays (fig. 4; Camuti and Riel, 1996; Monti and Fazakerley, 1997). For the main weathered horizons of saprolite, smectite, and limonite, the mineralogy includes serpentine±chlorite, smec-tite, opal, magnetite, talc, and dolomite; smectite±chlorite, serpentine, opal, quartz, serpentine, Fe-oxides, and oxyhy-droxides; and goethite and hematite±kaolinite, respectively (Camuti and Riel, 1996; Monti and Fazakerley, 1997; Wells, 2003; Gaudin and others, 2005).

The developed profile is locally influenced by faulting and shearing, but most of the variation in the profile mineral-ogy can be directly correlated to the underlying lithology,

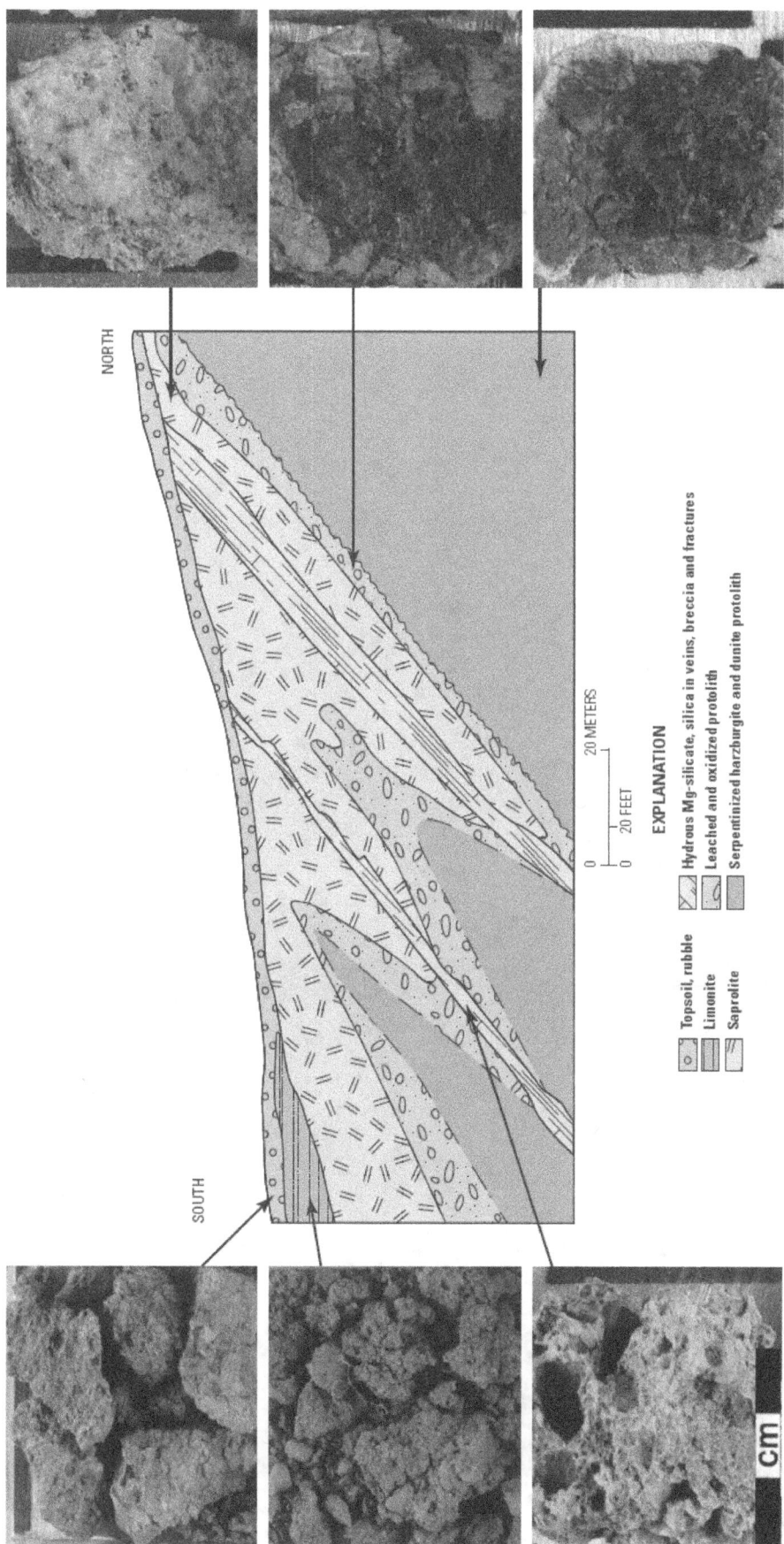

Figure 2. Cross section of an idealized laterite profile from Nickel Mountain, Riddle, Oregon, United States, with photographs of hand-specimen samples of (counterclockwise) topsoil, limonite, silica veins and breccia, serpentinized protolith, leached-oxidized protolith, and saprolite. Profile adapted from Data Metallogenica (2008) (*http://www.datametallogenica.com/*); photographs from Data Metallogenica by Peter Laznicka (1980). (Mg, magnesium)

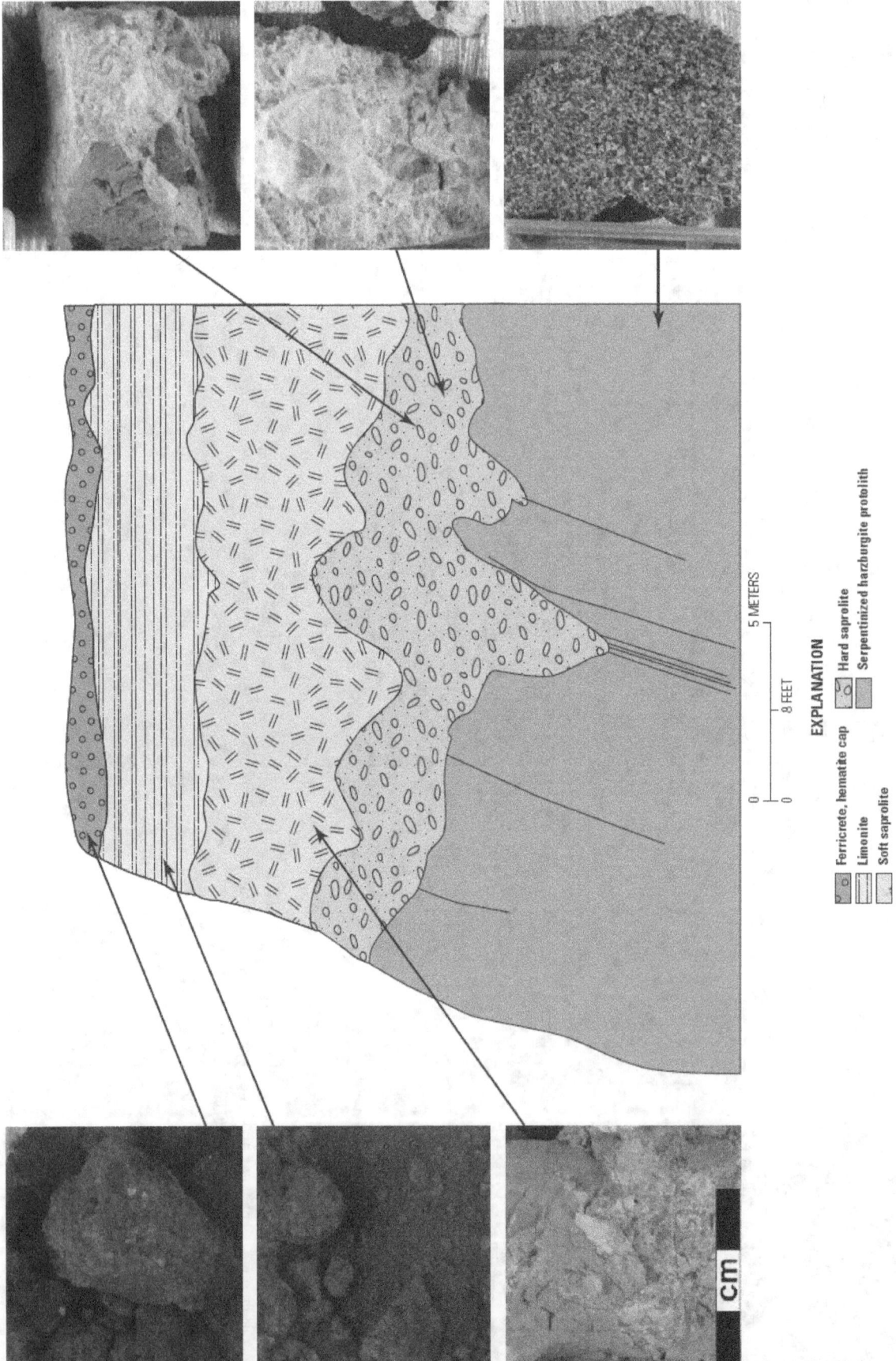

Figure 3. Cross section of an idealized laterite profile from the Falcondo district in the Dominican Republic of Hispaniola with photographs of hand-specimen samples of (counterclockwise) ferricrete, hematite cap; limonite; soft saprolite; serpentinized harzburgite; and (last two images) hard saprolite with poorly crystalline garnierite veinlets and breccia cement. Profile adapted from Data Metallogenica (2008) (*http://www.datametallogenica.com/*); photographs from Data Metallogenica by Peter Laznicka (1980).

EXPLANATION

Ferricrete, hematite cap   Hard saprolite

Limonite   Serpentinized harzburgite protolith

Soft saprolite

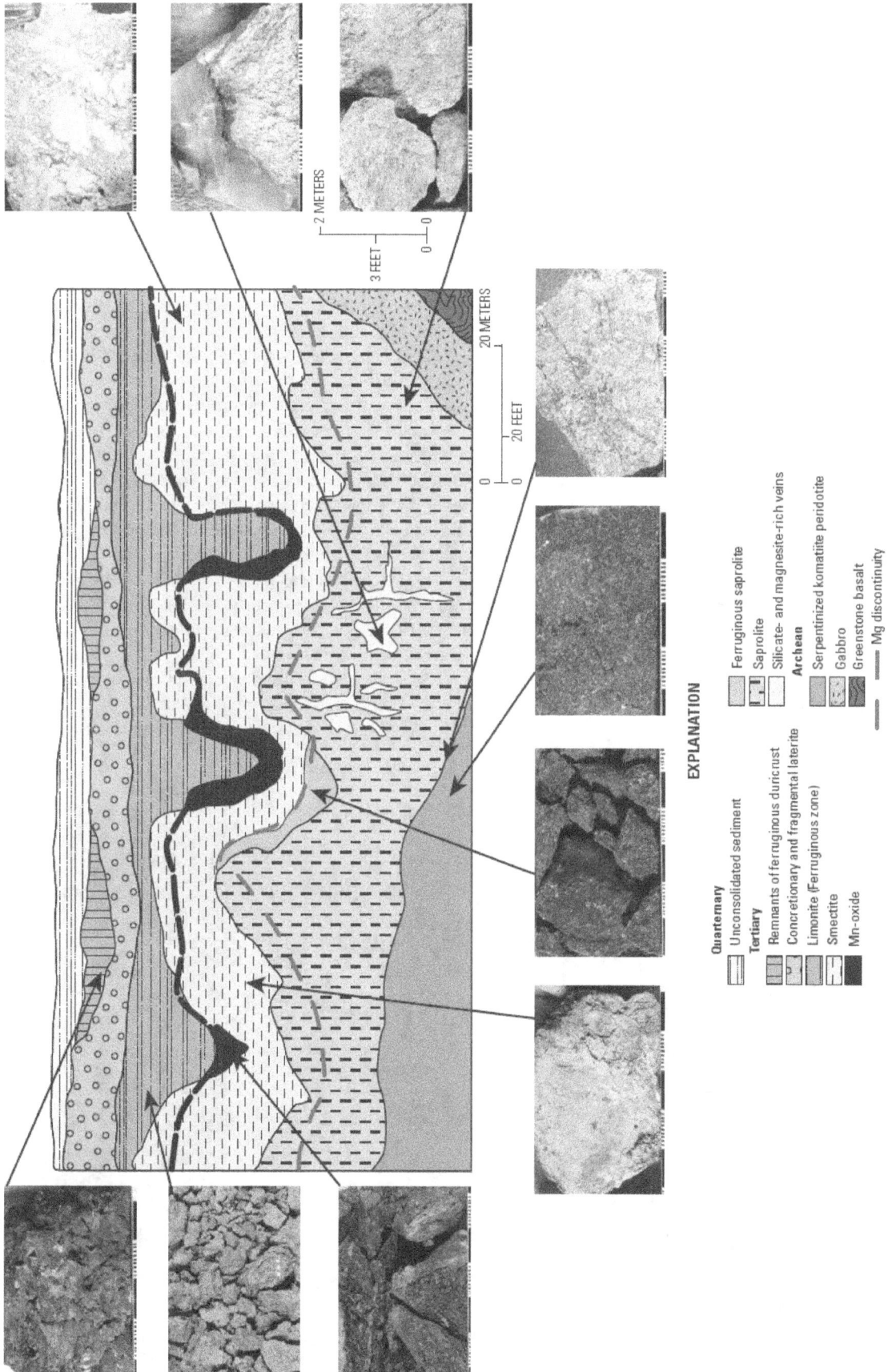

Figure 4.   Cross section of an idealized laterite profile from Murrin Murrin, Western Australia, Australia, with photographs of hand-specimen samples of (counterclockwise) ferruginous duricrust, limonite, manganese (Mn)-oxide, smectite, ferruginous saprolite, serpentinized komatiite peridotite, leached serpentinized komatiite peridotite, saprolite, chrysoprase in a silicate- and magnesite-rich veins. Profile adapted from Data Metallogenica (2008) (*http://www.datametallogenica.com/*); photographs from Data Metallogenica by Peter Laznicka (1980). (Mg, magnesium)

EXPLANATION

Quaternary
Unconsolidated sediment

Tertiary
Remnants of ferruginous duricrust

Concretionary and fragmental laterite

Limonite (Ferruginous zone)

Smectite

Mn-oxide

Ferruginous saprolite

Saprolite

Silicate- and magnesite-rich veins

Archean
Serpentinized komatiite peridotite

Gabbro

Greenstone basalt

Mg discontinuity

where aluminum (Al)-rich orthocumulates develop more chlorite and therefore thicker clay zones (Wells and Butt, 2006; see the section "Weathering/Supergene Processes" in this report, p. 20). The highest Ni concentrations (as much as 2.5 percent Ni; Gaudin and others, 2005) are in the clay zone. The Co occurs in Mn-oxides in the limonite zone and upper part of the clay zone. Unlike many other Ni-Co laterites, there is no garnierite at Murrin Murrin, which may be due to the parent rock at Murrin Murrin being entirely serpentinized (Gaudin and others, 2005) and possibly the relatively poor drainage of the Yilgarn craton. In deposits in Indonesia, for example, Golightly (1981) speculated that garnierite is only present where the parent rock is fresh to partially serpentinized, which may explain its absence in Western Australia.

Moa Bay, Cuba

In general, Ni laterite deposits in northeastern Cuba are oxide subtype (Gleeson and others, 2003). As with many Ni laterite districts, there are areas of exceptions in northeastern Cuba where hydrous Mg-silicate is the main ore type (Proenza and others, 2007). Because the dominant ore-processing method in Moa Bay is HPAL, it is difficult to treat the hydrous Mg-silicate subtype ore because Mg consumes acid in this process, making it uneconomical (Golightly and others, 2008).

The Moa Bay district is along the north coast of eastern Cuba. The measured and indicated metal resource for 2010 was reported as 66.60 Mt with a grade of 1.26 percent Ni and 0.13 percent Co and a proven and probable reserve of 47.77 Mt with a grade of 1.19 percent Ni and 0.13 percent Co (Beaton and others, 2011). The oxide subtype deposits in Moa Bay developed from the weathering of serpentinized peridotites (harzburgite), as well as dunite, of the Mayari-Baracoa ophiolite belt, which prior to weathering contained 0.2 percent Ni (de Vletter, 1955; Roqué-Rosell and others, 2010). In an environment of low relief and heavy rainfall, the olivine, clinopyroxene, and antigorite of the partially serpentinized ultramafic rocks were gradually leached of their most soluble elements, Mg and silicon (Si), whereas the less-soluble components, Fe, Ni, Co, Al, and Cr, were enriched.

A weathering profile containing economic amounts of Ni and Co formed in a continuous process and caused the zone of enrichment to progressively move down through the weathering profile (de Vletter, 1955; Lelong and others, 1976). At the Yagrumaje oxide-subtype Ni laterite deposit in Moa Bay, the laterite profile consists of a ferricrete cap underlain by limonite containing goethite, maghemite, hematite, and gibbsite, as well as Mn-Ni-Co oxyhydroxides (fig. 5; Roqué and others, 2008). The limonite is underlain by saprolite consisting of lizardite, goethite, magnetite, maghemite, chromite, and hydrous Mg-silicates. Because some areas of the Moa Bay district have lower relief, Ni and Co have been enriched because of the lateral transportation and subsequent reweathering of lateritic material from higher elevation (Linchenat and Shirokova, 1964). In many of the laterite ore profiles of the Moa Bay district, saprolite is absent, due possibly to erosion during a long submarine stage or from the subsequent weathering of transported laterite (Linchenat and Shirokova, 1964; Golightly,

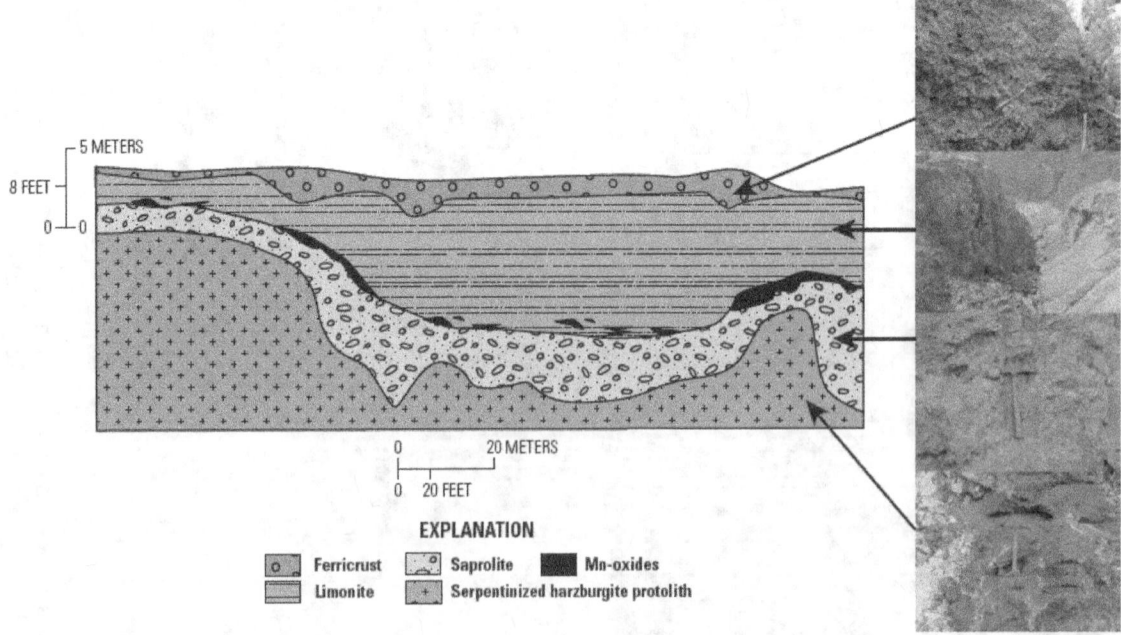

Figure 5. Idealized cross section through the nickel-cobalt laterite profile of Moa Bay, Cuba, with photographs of horizon examples of (from surface to base) ferricrust, limonite, saprolite, and protolith. Profile modified from Linchenat and Shirokova (1964); photomicrographs from Mosselmans and others (2008). (Mn, manganese)

2010). In some areas, a layer of rocky limonite occurs, which represents the erosional surface during a mid-Tertiary period when saprolite and limonite horizons were combined in a coastal and submarine erosional environment (Golightly and others, 2008). These layers overlie the protolith of serpentinized peridotite and harzburgite (Roqué-Rosell and others, 2010). The Mn-Ni-Co oxides occur in the lower part of the limonite zone as veins and coatings or concretions along fractures (de Vletter, 1955; Proenza and others, 2007). The Ni and Co are present in goethite (0.3–4.5 wt% Ni; 0.1–1.7 wt% Co), maghemite (0.5–8 wt% Ni; 1.1 wt% Co), and lithiophorite (less than or equal to 12 wt% Ni; 6 wt% Co) (Proenza and others, 2007).

Historical Evolution of Descriptive and Genetic Knowledge and Concepts

The term laterite was first defined by Buchanan (1807). The term is derived from the Latin word for brick and was used to describe the indurated clay in India, which Buchanan saw contained a large concentration of Fe that hardened upon surface exposure. Buchanan's application of the term is quite specific to material used for building. Depending on the perspective of the researcher, the term laterite has been applied to a variety of aspects of tropically weathered rocks. Laterite has been known as a variably cemented sesquioxide-rich soil and a surficial or near-surface reddish soil, as well as by an assortment of mineralogical definitions (Helgren and Butzer, 1977; Schellmann, 1986). The term has since developed to describe a profile in a tropically weathered regolith in which the most soluble elements are removed and the least soluble elements are progressively redistributed throughout a series of more to less weathered protoliths to form a concentrated deposit (Samama, 1986).

Regional Environment

Nickel-cobalt laterite deposits developed within 26 degrees of the equator with a few exceptions, such as the hydrous Mg-silicate deposit in Riddle, Oregon, and the laterite deposits in the Urals, Greece, and the Balkans.

Geotectonic Environment

The deposits are located in both presently active continental margins, in accreted terranes and obducted ophiolite sheets (New Caledonia; Moa Bay, Cuba; Falcondo, Dominican Republic) and in older accreted terranes and obducted ophiolites (Riddle, Oregon; Fifield, New South Wales; Brolga, Queensland), as well as in komatiite and cumulates that are now parts of stable cratons (Murrin Murrin, Western Australia; Goias, Brazil; Ambatovy, Madagascar) (Besairie and other,

1961; Colin and others, 1990; Windley and others, 1994; Bruce and others, 1998; Brand and others, 1998; Freyssinet and others, 2005; Platina Resources Limited, 2011).

Temporal (Secular) Relations

The global distribution of Ni-Co laterite deposits is a reflection of their ultramafic protolith and climate. Retallack (2010) gives a complete analysis of the secular variation of laterites. He describes the deposits as suffering from "the pull of recent," a concept discussed by Hay and Wood (1990) and Wilkinson and others (2009), because they are surface deposits and thus easily susceptible to denudation. Retallack (2010) notes that the formation of the laterite deposit initiated at approximately 2,300 million years ago (Ma), just subsequent to the onset of the first "Great Oxidation Event" (Rye and Holland, 1998), and that what were considered older laterites (approximately 3430 Ma; Ohmoto and others, 2007) are actually weathered banded Fe formations. Retallack (2010) also describes the importance of carbon dioxide (CO_2) in the process of hydrolytic weathering. He notes that laterite formation was scarce prior to 392 Ma because the high amount of CO_2 produced in rainforest soils was not present (Sheldon, 2006). The efficiency of rainforests to fix CO_2 in the soil can be seen in the drastic reduction in atmospheric CO_2 subsequent to the onset of rainforest development (see Royer and others, 2004, fig. 1). A combination of atmospheric CO_2 spikes and paleoclimatic fluctuations occurred during the development of the deposits that formed far from the equator, such as those in Oregon and the Ural Mountains (Retallack, 2010). As for the deposits in Australia, continental drift moved them from tropical regions to their more arid present-day locations.

Duration of Mineralizing Processes

The time required for the formation of a Ni-Co laterite deposit depends on the rate of weathering, the tectonic stability, and the rates of mechanical erosion. The rate of weathering depends on the amount of rainfall and evaporation in a region, which determines the amount of water infiltrating the laterite profile each year (Nahon and Tardy, 1992). The amount of rainfall and the proficiency of drainage help determine the extent of the development of the weathered profile. The thickness of the profile depends on how the weathering front and rate of erosion progress and the time in which these processes are allowed to develop (Elias, 2002). Calculating the rate of weathering requires an understanding of the hydrology and the effects of leaching on a profile (Nahon, 1982, 1986; Nahon and Tardy, 1992). Rates of chemical weathering for felsic, intermediate and ultramafic rocks are listed in table 2. Trescases (1973) and Leprun (1979) stressed that the rate of weathering for ultramafic rocks was about two to three times that of felsic rocks. The rate of weathering in stable tectonic environments is about 10 meters per million years (m/m.y.) (Golightly, 1981). In more active tectonic settings, the rate of profile development may reach about 50 m/m.y. (Golightly, 2010).

Table 2.   Rate of weathering for felsic and ultramafic rocks.

[m/m.y., meters per million years]

Rock type	Location	Weathering rate (m/m.y.)	Reference
Felsic	Ivory Coast	5–55	Leneuf (1959)
Felsic	Ivory Coast	14	Boulangé (1984)
Felsic	Chad	13.5	Gac (1979)
Felsic	Norway	12	Tardy (1969)
Felsic	France	10–24	Tardy (1969)
Felsic	Ivory Coast	15	Tardy (1969)
Felsic	Madagascar	25	Tardy (1969)
Intermediate	Puerto Rico, ridgetop	211	Buss and White (2012)
Intermediate	Puerto Rico, watershed	43–58	Buss and White (2012)
Ultramafic	New Caledonia	29–47	Trescases (1973)
Ultramafic		10–50	Elias (2002)
Ultramafic	New Caledonia, highlands	125–140	Trescases (1975)
Ultramafic	New Caledonia, plateaus and terraces	12.5–14	Trescases (1975)
Ultramafic	Stable craton	10	Golightly (1981)
Ultramafic	Tropical highlands	50	Golightly (2010)

Regionally, the results of these interplaying factors can be seen in the thick profiles of Western Australia, where there was a prolonged period of temperate to tropical weathering but little uplift and thus limited surface erosion with poor drainage. Resulting stunted development of the weathered profile included little or no saprolite and lower grade clay or oxide subtype ore. Therefore, these deposits are quite thick but of a lower grade. In active tectonic settings, such as New Caledonia, there is a high rate of weathering and continued uplift coupled with a high rate of surface erosion allowing for good drainage, which leads to the complete development of the higher grade, hydrous Mg-silicate subtype ores. The local geomorphic landscape affects the rate of development of a profile in an active tectonic setting because it controls rates of mechanical weathering, drainage of percolating water, and level of groundwater. For example, the rate of weathering in the highlands of New Caledonia is faster than on the plateaus and terraces (125–140 and 12.5–14 m/m.y., respectively; Trescases, 1975; Elias, 2002).

Golightly (1981) estimated the rate of chemical weathering from the amount of Mg and Si in the surface water from lateritic terranes. He showed that a substantial Ni-Co laterite ore deposit could develop in as little as one million years in an island arc setting, but it would take about 10 times as long on stable cratons; in both cases, the complete development of the profile probably takes longer. The durations of the weathering events that produced Ni-Co laterite deposits are summarized in figure 6. In the cratonic setting, protoliths for Ni-Co laterites have been exposed to weathering for long periods. For example, Western Australia and Brazil have ultramafic rocks within their cratons that have been exposed throughout the Phanerozoic (fig. 6) and likely for much longer. Buried or fossil laterite deposits in Greece and the Urals formed from the Devonian into the Cretaceous and were preserved below overlying sedimentary rock sequences. More recently formed deposits in an active tectonic setting in the southeast Pacific and the Caribbean formed from the Eocene to the present (Freyssinet and others, 2005).

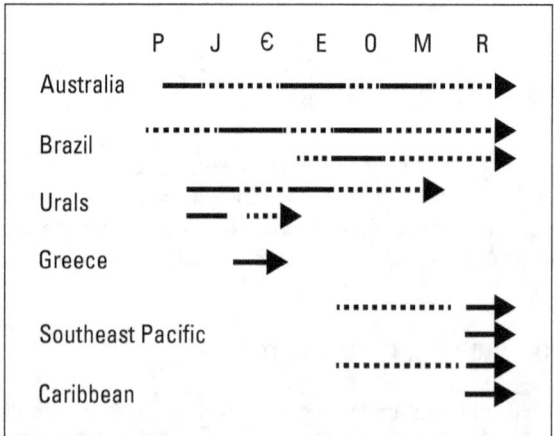

Figure 6.   Periods of nickel-cobalt laterite formation in various locations. Solid and dashed lines represent the periods of principal weathering and minor alteration, respectively. Modified from Freyssinet and others (2005). (P, Paleozoic; J, Jurassic; Є, Cretaceous; E, Eocene; O, Oligocene; M, Miocene; R, Recent)

Relations to Structures

Structures, faults, and fractures, as well as joints and cleavage, can play a key role in the development of Ni-Co laterite deposits. One of the most important factors in forming Ni-Co laterite deposits is the degree of permeability of the parent material (Norton, 1973; de Vletter, 1978). Structure controls Ni mineralization and weathering (Pelletier, 1996). Faults and shears increase the permeability of the protolith in well-drained and saturated profile scenarios (Elias, 2002; Golightly, 2010). Faults also play a key role in Ni-Co laterite mineralization in the Urals where some deposits occur along steeply dipping faults in serpentinite protoliths. Rather than the traditional horizontal progression of weathering horizons, these deposits have a zonation dependent on the proximity to faults (Jubelt, 1956). Laznicka (1985) speculated that these linear-type deposits in the Urals are remnants of blanketed deposits that have been eroded away. Faults allow for pervasive circulation of water through susceptible protolith, developing limonite and saprolite alteration layers that are greater than 3 kilometers (km) in length, 80 meters (m) in width, and 120 m in depth, such as the Nowo-Akkermann deposits (fig. 7; Jubelt, 1956; de Vletter, 1978).

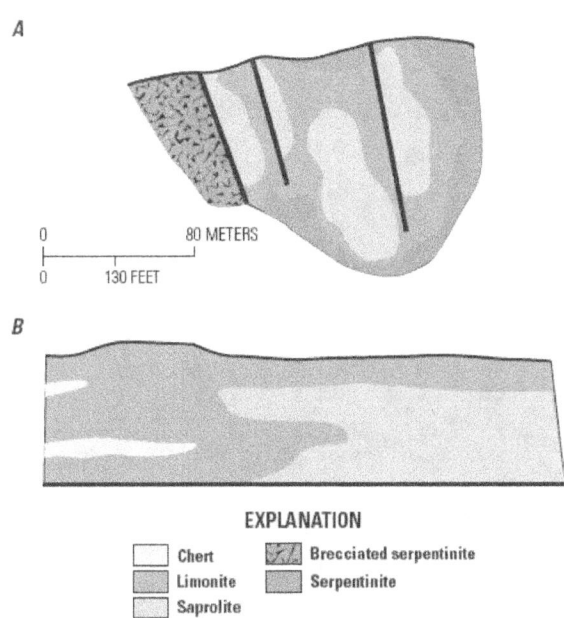

Figure 7. Perpendicular cross sections through the Nowo-Akkermann deposit, Russia. *A,* The weathering zonation occurs as a function of the proximity to the faults, rather than the traditional horizontal differentiation of the weathering horizons. *B,* Longitudinal cross section through an ore zone proximal to a fault. Modified from Jubelt (1956).

Fluid follows fractures and intricacies of the cracked protolith along a path of least resistance, causing the boundaries between weathering layers in a profile to be highly irregular (de Vletter, 1955). The structurally and texturally influenced increase in permeability causes enrichment along fissures, settling of boulders, and rim enrichment of the protolith fragments, such that deposit complexity can stem from the structure in the protolith (de Vletter, 1955). The morphology of the profile is heavily influenced by the extent of the development of the tectonic features; the better developed the fracturing and brecciation, the deeper the weathering front (Samama, 1986). Golightly (1981) noted that the rate of development of a Ni-Co laterite profile is controlled by joint spacing (see Golightly, 1981, fig. 16), and Elias (2002) stated that joints and cleavage allow for pervasive percolation of water and greater potential for alteration. At the Cawse deposit in Australia, secondary structures and localized shear zones influence development of the weathering profile because they provide the initial permeability for water to penetrate the protolith, leading to alteration and secondary enrichment (Brand and others, 1998). Wells (2003) noted that the development of the laterite profile at Murrin Murrin in Australia is locally influenced by faulting and shearing.

Fractures are important to ore control. Saprolite developed on unserpentinized dunites is composed of mostly rich garnierite ores that rim barren dunite boulders and fill fractures and voids. This type of ore can be upgraded easily by screening (Samama, 1986). For example, in Soroako, Indonesia, ore is upgraded by milling the saprolite from the rims of the unserpentinized harzburgite corestones (Golightly, 1979a).

Relations to Igneous Rocks

The Ni-Co laterites develop from the pervasive chemical and mechanical weathering of ultramafic igneous rocks and serpentinite. Generally, two classes of ultramafic rocks can produce an economic Ni-Co laterite deposit if exposed to prolonged weathering: (1) dunite, peridotite, harzburgite, and wehrlite in Alpine-type ophiolite sequences and in large thrust sheets of obducted ophiolites, and (2) olivine dominant komatiites and mafic-ultramafic layered intrusions, which are present within many Precambrian shields (Brand and others, 1998). When an ultramafic magma cools, Ni and Co tend to fractionate into the lattice of olivine and pyroxene, respectively.

Globally, 15 percent of the known Ni-Co laterites develop from the weathering of komatiites and layered mafic-ultramafic intrusions, and 85 percent develop from dunites, harzburgites, and peridotites in accretionary terranes (Brand and others, 1998; Elias, 2006). On a local scale, variation in the primary lithology can influence the ore subtype. For example, the Australia clay subtype ores at Bulong and Murrin Murrin developed from olivine orthocumulate; the oxide subtype deposit at Cawse developed from an olivine meso-adcumulate (Brand and others, 1998).

Relations to Sedimentary Rocks

Sedimentary rocks are present as cover sequences that preserve Ni-Co laterite deposits in Albania and Greece. These deposits are lithified, tilted, and folded. Some of these deposits, as well as various deposits in the Urals, formed from the subsequent transport of in situ laterite concentrations. In Greece and Albania, oxide and hydrous Mg-silicate subtype Ni-Co laterite deposits developed from the pervasive weathering of ultramafic rocks of an ophiolite nappe emplaced in the Jurassic. These deposits were subsequently covered in the Cretaceous by shallow water limestone and, in some locations, molasse, thus preserving the Ni-Co laterite mineralization. The cover restricted surficial weathering, and associated burial allowed for reconcentration of the residual elements by low-grade metamorphism (Valeton and others, 1987).

Relations to Metamorphic Rocks

The primary alteration of ultramafic rocks by regional metamorphism results in serpentinization. This initial alteration enhances the development of Ni-Co laterite deposits because the metamorphic mineralogy and textures are conducive to pervasive chemical and mechanical weathering. Refer to the section "Petrology of Associated Metamorphic Rocks" on p. 25 for further discussion.

The ores in Greece, Albania, and the Urals have been metamorphosed to as high as amphibolite facies subsequent to Ni-Co laterite formation (Mposkos, 1981; Valeton and others, 1987; Economou-Eliopoulos, 2003; Zevgolis and others, 2010; M. Economou-Eliopoulos, cited by J.P. Golightly, Golightly Geoscience, written commun., 2012). Although these Ni-Co laterites have been metamorphosed, the Ni grade is similar to the in situ deposits (1.02–1.3 percent Ni; Berger and others, 2011)

Physical Description of Deposit

Dimensions in Plan View

The average area of the Ni-Co laterite deposits that have been mined is about 24 square kilometers (km²) (fig. 8; Berger and others, 2011). The largest and smallest reported areas of the economic deposits are 188 and 0.16 km², respectively (Berger and others, 2011).

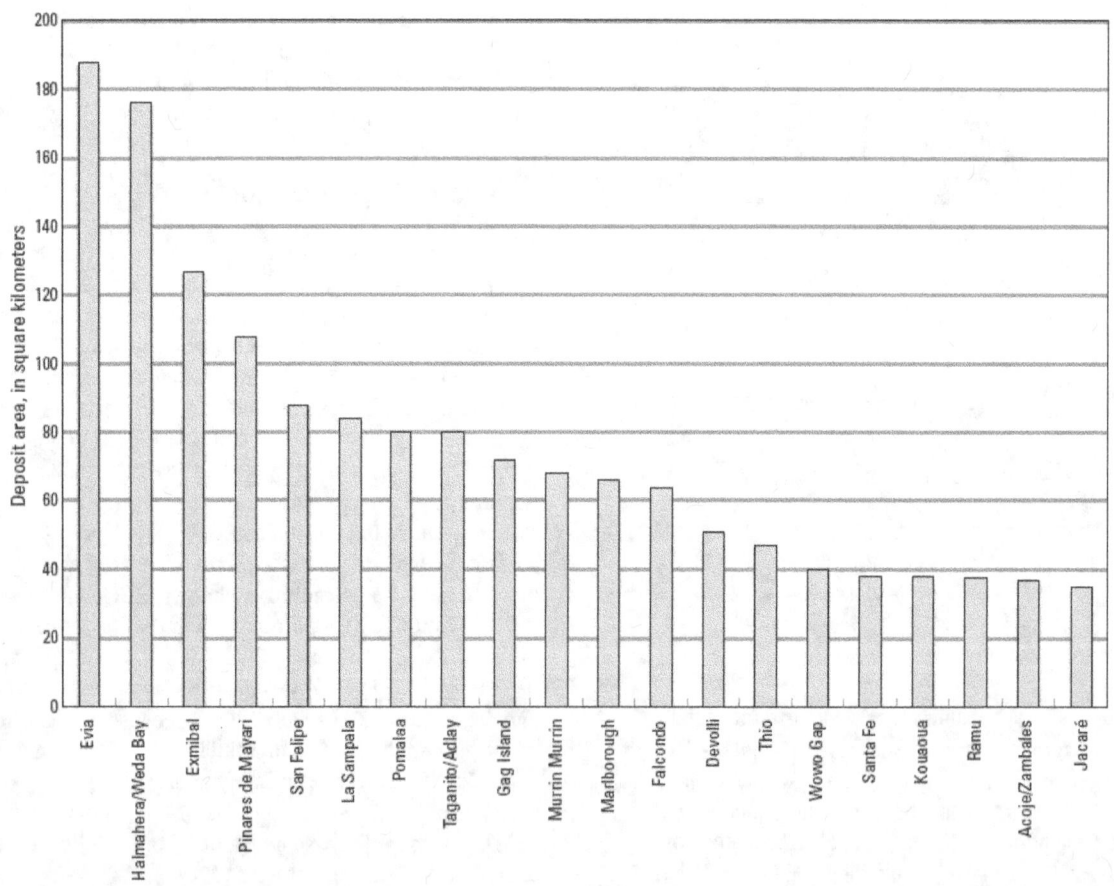

Figure 8. Deposit areas for the 20 largest exploited nickel-cobalt laterite deposits (see fig. 1 for deposit locations). Compiled from Berger and others (2011).

Vertical Extent and Form/Shape

In general, Ni-Co laterites are laterally extensive deposits, with dimensions as much as 28 km in length (Berger and others, 2011). They are in the form of a weathered profile (fig. 9); tectonic setting, geomorphology, and structure are key controls on the physical properties of Ni-Co laterite deposits. The Ni-Co laterites range in thickness from a few meters to several tens of meters (Golightly, 1981). The variable thickness of the Ni-bearing ores stems from the nature of the weathering process occurring along weaknesses in the parent rock forming an uneven contact with the saprolite horizon (see Golightly, 1981, fig. 16). Where porosity and permeability are high, the profile is thickest, and where the profile is thickest, the grades of Ni and Co are higher (Elias, 2006).

Host Rocks

The Ni-Co laterites most commonly form above ultramafic igneous rocks that have undergone varying degrees of serpentinization (see the sections "Relations to Igneous Rocks," p. 11, and "Relations to Metamorphic Rocks," p. 12). Because the laterites form from the pervasive weathering of the ultramafic rocks, the degree of weathering of the protolith places the initial constraint on the shape and size of the deposit. The laterites can also occur above sediments, such as the extensively transported limestone-based laterites in Greece and Albania, or on other types of igneous rocks, such as some of the deposits in Brazil that are laterites redeposited from erosion of the surrounding ultramafic plateau (Trescases and others, 1979; Eliopoulos and Economou-Eliopoulos, 2000). Nickel-cobalt laterites formed from accreted ophiolite sequences are restricted by the preservation potential in tectonically active regions. Those that formed from weathering of cumulates in more stable cratonic environments may be more laterally extensive because the lack of uplift in a region prevents the mechanical weathering of a laterite profile, creating a single planation surface (Samama, 1986). Geomorphological setting affects the size and shape of the deposits because they can form on summits, plateaus, and slopes as blankets of regolith.

Structural Setting and Control

In rare cases, Ni-Co laterites form linear deposits along major structures, such as the fault-hosted deposit in the Urals (Glaskovsky and others, 1977). In some regions, the laterite deposits have been elongated by years of displacement along major structures. At a deposit scale, structure controls the pervasiveness of the weathering into the parent lithology (see Golightly, 1981, fig. 16).

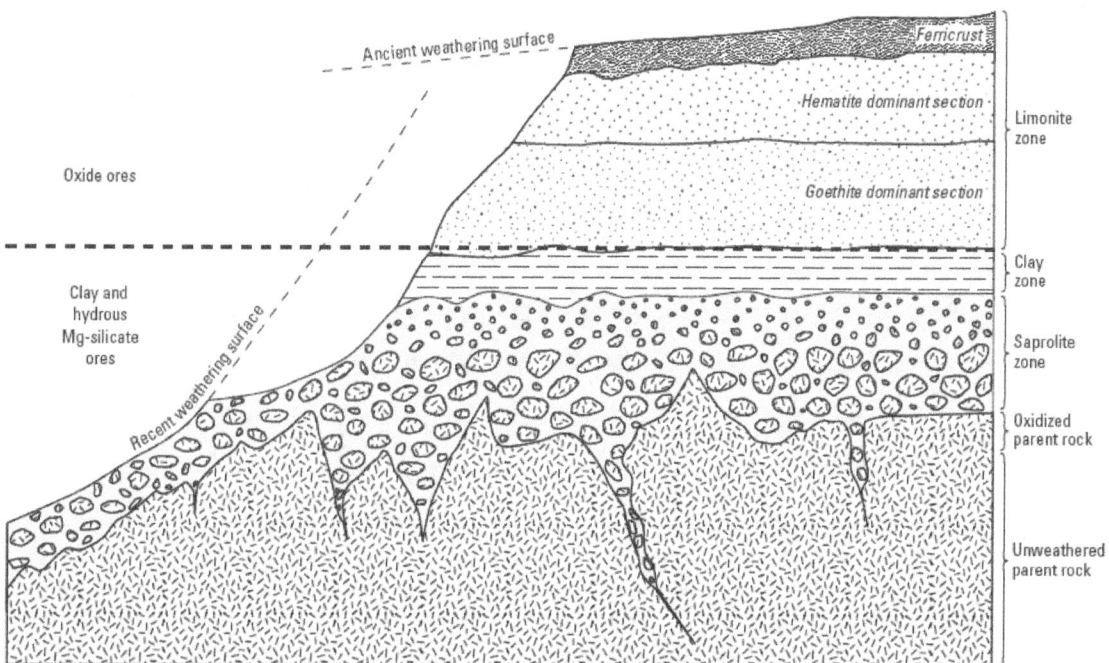

Figure 9.   Idealized cross section through a nickel laterite weathered profile illustrating all the possible layers. Natural profiles are more complex and contain diverse sequences of any or all of the layers shown. Modified from Samama (1986). (Mg, magnesium)

Geophysical Characteristics

Modern geophysical methods employed at multiple scales can be useful during exploration for Ni-Co laterite deposits. At a regional scale, aeromagnetic, radiometric, gravity, and optical remote-sensing techniques provide insight into the broad crustal framework in which Ni-Co laterite deposits may be hosted. These methods are effective for mapping ultramafic and serpentinized rocks, as well as their weathered products. In addition, gravity and magnetic methods can be used to map fault zones. At a deposit scale, magnetic, gravity, electromagnetic, electrical, and ground-penetrating radar (GPR) methods can be useful in delineating the weathering profile in which Ni-Co laterite deposits form. Interpretation of these data is non-unique and, therefore, should be constrained with independent information, such as geologic mapping and drilling, or multiple geophysical techniques.

Magnetic and Gravity Methods

Aeromagnetic data provide information on the distribution of magnetic minerals, mainly magnetite. The magnetic property of a rock is quantified by its magnetic susceptibility. In general, rocks with larger concentrations of magnetite have high magnetic susceptibilities and produce magnetic anomaly highs when compared to rocks with low magnetic susceptibilities. Mafic and ultramafic igneous rocks tend to have higher magnetic susceptibilities and produce stronger magnetic anomaly highs relative to felsic igneous rocks (table 3). In general, the magnetic technique can be an important tool for Ni-Co exploration because small ultramafic bodies that have been serpentinized can be distinguished from other lithologies by the magnetic signature of magnetite associated with serpentinization. The Ni-rich olivine core zones of komatiitic flows tend to be anomalous for the same reason.

Patterns in aeromagnetic anomaly maps can be used to infer the distribution of geologic units and are particularly useful where bedrock is concealed by unconsolidated material or vegetation. With Ni-Co laterite deposits commonly found in tropical climates, where vegetation is abundant, this technique can prove particularly useful. The Ni-Co laterite deposits form as the result of complex weathering of serpentinized mafic and ultramafic rocks. During serpentinization, the ultramafic rocks are hydrated and oxidized. Such processes commonly result in the formation of magnetite. If magnetite forms in concentrations that are high enough, a positive magnetic anomaly will be produced, although differentiating such anomalies from those produced by nearby ultramafic rocks, if present, is difficult. Subsequent geologic processes can destroy the magnetite, and the serpentinite may be represented as magnetic anomaly lows. Therefore, interpretation of magnetic anomalies associated with serpentinized rock is complex.

Studies in northeastern Cuba provide a good example of the use of magnetic data in targeting lateritic ores. The Ni-Co laterite deposits are within the 170-km-long Mayarí-Baracoa ophiolite belt that consists of two complexes, the Mayarí-Nicaro to the west and the Moa-Baracoa to the east. The

Table 3.   Physical properties of some common rock types associated with nickel-cobalt laterite deposits (Peric, 1981; Ford and others, 2008).

[g/cm³, grams per cubic centimeter; %, percent; ppm, parts per million; mS/m, millisiemens per centimeter]

Rock type	Magnetic susceptibility (SI*10⁻³)	Density (g/cm³)	Radioelement			Conductivity[1] (mS/m)
			Potassium (%)	Uranium (ppm)	Thorium (ppm)	
Limestone	0.3	2.6	0.3	2	1.3	0.01–1
Dolomite	0.1	2.7				0.01–1
Laterite crust			0.4	1.9	3.4	
Saprolite (mafic volcanic rocks, schist)						50–500
Saprolite (felsic volcanic rocks, granite, gneiss)						
Felsic igneous rocks	8	2.6	3.4	4.5	25.7	
Mafic igneous rocks	25	2.8	0.8	0.8	2.3	
Basalt	70	3.0	0.7	0.8	2.2	0.2
Gabbro	70	3.0	0.4	1.4	1.7	0.0
Hornblende gabbro		3.1				
Peridotite	250	3.2				1.7
Pyroxenite	125	3.2				
Serpentinite	3–17	2.8	0.4	1.7	2.3	8

[1]Conductivity is the inverse of resistivity.

ophiolites were tectonically emplaced on volcano-sedimentary rocks. The typical ophiolite sequence constitutes serpentinized peridotite overlain by gabbros. At a regional scale, the comparison of geology and magnetic anomaly maps shows the strongest positive magnetic anomalies are associated with the thickest ophiolitic rocks, and the negative anomalies were attributed to volcano-sedimentary rocks and areas where hydrothermal alteration occurred subsequent to the emplacement of the ophiolitic belt (Batista-Rodríguez, 2006). Three-dimensional inversions of the magnetic field data constrained by magnetic susceptibility measurements and mapped geology provided thickness estimates for the ophiolite rocks and volcano-sedimentary rock units in the region and suggested prospecting targets where thin layers of serpentinized peridotites overlie basement (Batista-Rodríguez and others, 2007). The inversions also correlated well with mapped faults and suggested the presence of new faults not previously mapped or observed. At a deposit scale, aeromagnetic data can be used to help develop the three-dimensional geologic framework. Using complex transformations of the magnetic field that include horizontal gradients, vertical gradients, and upward continuation led to a better understanding of the subsurface geometry of ultramafic rocks (Batista-Rodríguez, 2006). Magnetic anomaly highs were attributed to thicker sections of the ultramafic rocks. Known Ni-Co laterite deposits correlated with magnetic anomaly lows and suggested thin serpentinized bodies in outlying areas of the ophiolite massif or tectonic uplift, where erosion has removed overlying gabbroic units (Batista-Rodríguez, 2006).

Gravity data measure the variations in the gravity field that result from differing densities of underlying material. In general, igneous rocks have higher densities than sedimentary rocks, and mafic igneous rocks tend to have higher densities than felsic rocks (table 3). During serpentinization, large amounts of water are absorbed into the rocks. This process increases the volume of the rocks and decreases the density from 3.3 to 2.7 grams per cubic centimeter (g/cm^3). This density contrast can potentially be imaged in a high-resolution gravity survey and thereby help direct exploration efforts. Forward modeling using gravity and magnetic data constrained by physical property values and known geology can help determine the thickness of the weathered profile and help establish favorable areas for exploration.

Radiometric Method

Airborne radiometric surveys, also known as gamma-ray spectrometry, measure the concentrations of potassium (K), uranium (U), and thorium (Th) in the upper few centimeters of the surface of the Earth. The abundances are measured by detecting the gamma rays produced during their natural radioactive decay. These elements are the three most abundant naturally occurring radioactive elements present in various proportions in all rocks and soils. In general, mafic and ultramafic rocks have lower concentrations of K, U, and Th than felsic rocks (table 3). Weathering of all rock types leads to loss of K, and for felsic rocks, loss of U and Th as well, whereas weathering of intermediate through ultramafic rocks may result in enrichment of U and Th (Dickson and Scott, 1997). The U increase may be the result of adsorption in clays and precipitation of Fe-oxides, whereas Th is relatively stable during weathering.

The distribution of the radioelements provides clues to the understanding of the geology. Unfortunately, freestanding water and moisture in soils and transported materials can mask the radioelement response, so care must be taken when conducting surveys in tropical environments typically favorable for laterite formation. It is important to note that a measured point from airborne data is an average element concentration over a larger surface area, so absolute localized concentration measurements are not possible unless one uses a ground instrument. Depending on the survey design, mainly the line spacing, these data can be examined either on a profile basis or by concentrations gridded as a continuous surface. The data should be interpreted in terms of surface chemistry.

In general, because ultramafic rocks cause a strong negative radiometric anomaly, an airborne radiometric survey can be useful for finding ultramafic rocks in deeply weathered areas, as in the recent discoveries of the Serra dos Tapas and Vale dos Sonhos Ni-Co laterite deposits in Brazil (Golightly, 2010). In addition, radiometric data over the allochthonous Mayarí-Baracoa ophiolitic belt of northeastern Cuba enhanced the understanding of Ni-Co laterite formation and distribution (Batista and others, 2008). The lateritic soils showed elevated concentrations of U and Th. In places where laterites were redeposited, the element concentrations were even greater. A correlation was shown between high concentrations of U and Th over thicker, more developed or redeposited laterites that overlay serpentinized ultramafic rocks.

Optical Remote Sensing Method

Optical remote sensing measures the way in which incident light from the sun reflects off surface material. In mineral exploration, the measured wavelengths typically range from visible to shortwave infrared regions of the electromagnetic spectrum. Generally, in the relation between wavelength and reflectance, various lithologic units and minerals yield a unique spectra with diagnostic absorption features. The spectra of the target material can be compared to spectral libraries, and a material identification can be made. Hyperspectral data have narrow and contiguous spectral bands, providing greater certainty in material identification. These data can be costly and typically are not readily available. Multispectral data have wider spectral bands and can be useful in distinguishing alteration mineral groups such as hydrous clays and Fe-oxides. These data are relatively inexpensive and are nearly global in coverage. Multispectral images readily detect lateral variations in surface material and cover large swaths of land on the order of thousands of square kilometers. Landsat and ASTER (Advanced Spaceborne Thermal Emission and Reflection Radiometer) contain six and nine spectral bands, respectively, from the visible to shortwave infrared region of the electromagnetic spectrum. One drawback of optical remote sensing is that it only measures surficial material and may not be optimal in highly vegetated areas, a considerable drawback when exploring for Ni-Co laterites in tropical regions.

During exploration, hyperspectral scanning and infrared spectroscopy can be used for preliminary determination of mineralogy. During production, these techniques can be used as tools for orebody definition and grade control (Freyssinet and others, 2005). Wells and Chia (2011) combine geochemical and hyperspectral scanning data, using partial least-squares regression, to predict Ni content in oxide subtype ores. Basile and others (2010) tried to quantify the amount of serpentinite in Ni-Co laterite profiles using diffuse reflectance infrared Fourier transform spectroscopy (FTIR) and multivariate statistical analysis. Such information is useful for maximizing ore processing because serpentinite, although host to substantial amounts of Ni, consumes acid during leaching.

Multispectral imagery has proven useful for Ni-Co laterite exploration in the Conceição do Araguaia region of the Araguaia belt in Brazil (Sícoli Seoane and others, 2009). The Araguaia belt is part of the Neoproterozoic Paraguai-Araguaia orogeny that formed as cratons collided during the assembly of West Gondwana. Ophiolite fragments within the belt were thrust over metasedimentary rocks. The ophiolites are composed of serpentinized peridotites and pods of dunite, talc schists, tremolite-actinolite schists (harzburgites), massive basalts, and pillow basalts. Weathering has been ongoing since early Tertiary. Advanced image processing techniques were applied to ASTER imagery and successfully mapped prospective mineral alteration and key mineral groups (Sícoli Seoane and others, 2009). The mineral groups included serpentine, pyrophyllite, smectite (±kaolinite), chlorite, kaolinite, amorphous silica, and limonite. The results of the ASTER mapping also demonstrate various Ni-bearing simple oxides of the periclase group, multiple oxides of the spinel group, and telluride and phosphates that represent potential minerals for vectoring Ni mineralization and are detectable in multispectral images.

Electrical Methods

Electrical methods, including electrical resistivity and electromagnetic (EM) techniques, respond to the electrical conductivity of rocks and minerals. Such measurements can span many orders of magnitude (table 3). Electrical resistivity surveys are achieved by injecting current into the ground using a pair of electrodes and measuring the voltage at another pair of electrodes. The induced polarization (IP) method measures the voltage decay (chargeability) after the current has been interrupted. Electromagnetic surveys are carried about by transmitting an EM field, which penetrates the ground and produces a secondary field when conductive material is encountered. The secondary field is then measured by a receiver. The technique can be performed in both the frequency and time domains.

Electrical resistivity methods were applied during exploration for Ni-Co laterite deposits in Burundi (Peric, 1981). Mafic and ultramafic rocks are aligned in a north-northeastern trend. The ultramafic rocks consist of harzburgite, wehrlite, and partially serpentinized dunite. Minor occurrences of pyroxenite are also present. The laterite profile consists of a limonite and saprolite zone overlying unweathered ultramafic rocks. The Ni concentrations are present at the base of the limonite zone and in the saprolite zone. Resistivity and IP logs mapped the different zones of the laterite profile. The limonite zone showed high resistivity attributed to magnetite content, whereas the saprolite zone showed low resistivity and chargeability attributed to high concentrations of clay subtype minerals. The underlying peridotites displayed a moderate resistivity. The electrical resistivity methods, complemented with a ground gravity survey, can be effective in mapping the laterite zone.

Airborne EM data have been used to better understand Ni-Co laterite deposits in Western Australia (Rutherford and others, 2001). The study utilized multiparameter borehole geophysical techniques and laboratory analysis of mineralogy, geochemistry, and soluble salt content to help constrain the airborne EM data. In the Yilgarn craton of Western Australia, olivine-rich cumulate rocks and their metamorphic derivatives have weathered to form nickeliferous laterite deposits. Rutherford and others (2001) demonstrated that the electrical response is indicative of a complex interplay between textural and mineralogical variations, acting in concert to control the movement of water through the regolith. The main constraints on electrical conductivity are related to the distribution and abundance of soluble salts and inferred presence of moisture in the unsaturated zone. Therefore, an understanding of hydrostratigraphic units is essential when interpreting airborne EM data while exploring for Ni-Co laterite deposits.

Ground-Penetrating Radar Method

Ground-penetrating radar (GPR) can be an effective tool for understanding the weathering profile where Ni-Co laterite deposits may be present. The method is effective where laterite thickness ranges from extremely thin to 50 m (Francké and Nobes, 2000). In tropical weathering profiles, GPR is sensitive to water content, conductivity, and Fe content (Francké and Nobes, 2000). Variations of the percentage of bound water present are a major controlling factor for the reflection of radar waves. Water can slow or impede the passage of radar waves. Unsaturated soil and limonite are porous material with relatively low bounding water; therefore, radar waves can travel at higher velocities. Radar waves travel at relatively low velocities through the saprolite zone, where clay minerals with high water content can concentrate. Radar waves travel at substantially higher velocities through rock because of a relatively low water content. Highly conductive materials, such as clays, can absorb radar energy and limit the depth of investigation. High concentrations of Fe can lead to reflections in horizontal bands.

In a series of studies, Francké and Nobes (2000) showed the effectiveness of GPR during the advanced phases of exploration at multiple Ni-Co laterite deposits. The studies showed that the GPR technique could clearly define the saprolite horizon in a laterite profile. The thickness of the weathered horizons in a laterite profile is highly variable, but the GPR technique provides a continuous image of the bedrock at depth, leading to a much higher resolution and a more complete projection of the orebody. The GPR technique is a cost effective tool that can detect troughs and pillars that are potentially missed by drilling programs.

Data Integration

Horton (2008) describes the necessity of achieving a comprehensive geologic understanding of laterite profiles for resource estimation by combining the traditional geologic techniques of mapping and drill-hole logging with geophysical tools such as GPR and high-resolution topographic data. In addition, interpreted geological information derived from other geophysical datasets should be considered. Magnetic and gravity data may lead to a better understanding of the bedrock geology. Radiometric data and optical remote sensing may provide infill information for geologic-mapping efforts and lead to a better understanding of surficial material. Electrical methods may help to understand the distribution of subsurface material with contrasting electrical properties. During exploration, hyperspectral scanning and infrared spectroscopy can be used initially to determine ore grade and mineralogy. During production, these techniques can be used as tools for orebody definition and grade control (Freyssinet and others, 2005). As Wells and Chia (2011) and Basile and others (2010) demonstrated, various geophysical

tools can be used to determine ore grade and distinguish mineralogy that can be detrimental to ore-processing proficiency. Evaluation and integration of these disparate datasets should lead to more reliable resource estimation.

Hypogene Ore Characteristics

Hypogene ore, gangue, or alteration characteristics are not associated with the Ni-Co laterite deposits because these are deposits formed in the weathering environment.

Supergene Ore and Gangue Characteristics

Mineralogy, Textures, Structures, and Grain Size

The fine-grained nature of minerals in Ni-Co laterite deposits requires more advanced analytical techniques for definitive identification than classic optical petrography. Traditionally, alteration sequences were interpreted from petrography, such as the work of Troly and others (1979) in New Caledonia. More modern research on deposits in Cuba and Australia, for example, uses X-ray diffraction, transmission electron microscopy–energy-dispersive X-ray spectroscopy (TEM-EDX), electron microprobe analysis, scanning electron microscope, hyperspectral scanning, and infrared spectroscopy to more definitively identify the laterite profile mineralogy (Gaudin and others, 2005; Proenza and others, 2007; Basile and others, 2010; Wells and Chia, 2011).

Table 4.   Nickel laterite terminology and general mineralogy. Adapted from Samama (1986) and Freyssinet and others (2005).

Ore type	Zone	Section	Alternative nomenclature	Nickel-bearing minerals
Oxide	Limonite	Pisolitic	Nodular ironstone, ferricrete layer, durricrust, iron pan, iron cap, canga, cuirasse	Geothite Hematite Asbolan Lithophorite Heterogenite
		Hematite dominant	Fine-grained saprolite, red laterite	
		Geothite dominant	In situ limonite zone, yellow laterite	
Silicate	Clay		Intermediate zone, smectite-quartz zone, quartz goethite zone, nontronite zone, mottle clay zone	Nontronite Beidellite Montmorillonite Saponite
	Hydrous Mg-silicate		Saprolite, serpentine ore, soft serpentine, soft saprolite, saprolitic serpentine, coarse grained saprolite	Serpentine group Talc group Chlorite group Sepiolite group Garnierite group
	Oxidized parent rock		Hard saprolite, saprolitic peridotite, saprock	

The parent rock consisting of olivine, which is highly unstable at near-surface conditions, and varying forms of serpentine (antigorite, chrysotile, lizardite, and brucite), depending on its previous alteration history, weathers to chlorite, talc, quartz, goethite, amorphous Fe-oxide, and silica. In the weathered profile, serpentine is enriched in Ni that substitutes in the lattice for Mg. Within the three mineralogical subtypes of Ni laterite deposits (oxide, clay, and hydrous Mg-silicate), more than 30 Ni-bearing minerals have been recognized (Brand and others, 1998; Gleeson and others, 2003; Freyssinet and others, 2005; Golightly, 2010). Their distribution as ore is not universal or consistent. Terms used to describe the progressively developed stages of weathering in a laterite profile are listed in table 4 along with their typical mineralogy.

The mineralogical paragenesis of a Ni laterite is a sequential process where over time, as the laterite profile develops, the mineralogy of the ultramafic parent rock weathers to hydrous Mg-silicates, clays, and oxides. Golightly (1981, 2010) demonstrated that the paragenesis of a Ni laterite profile could be explained with the solubility equilibrium of the minerals. The most soluble minerals, olivine and pyroxene, remain in the youngest, freshest part of the profile, whereas the least soluble, goethite, constitutes the most developed part of the profile (fig. 10). Increase of pH with depth in a profile allows for elements to be deposited as secondary enrichments. Thus, in general, mineralogy of a Ni laterite profile

can be separated by paragenetic sections or horizons within a weathered profile (fig. 10). The lower section consists of the unweathered protolith, such as fresh or primarily serpentinized dunite or peridotites (see the section "Relations to Igneous Rocks," p. 11). A saprolite layer consisting of remnants of the protolith and lizardite, goethite, magnetite, maghemite, chromite, and hydrous Mg- and Ni-rich silicates is above the protolith. The top of the saprolite transitions into a clay-rich layer that consists of smectite clays and amorphous silica, which forms in areas with restricted drainage, such as in many of the deposits in Western Australia. In areas where the profiles are well drained, such as in much of New Caledonia, this clay-rich layer does not develop. A limonite layer develops above with goethite, maghemite, hematite, gibbsite, and Mn-oxyhydroxides, such as lithiophorite and asbolane. The limonite generally consists of upper and lower zones. A hematite- and goethite-rich duricrust, called the ferricrete or iron cap, is at the top of the profile.

There are generally five groups of silicate minerals in the hydrous Mg-silicate subtype Ni laterite ore. These include the poorly crystalline garnierite group, sepiolite group, serpentine group, talc group, and chlorite group (table 4; Brand and others, 1998; Freyssinet and others, 2005).

Nontronite, beidellite, montmorillonite, and saponite make up the Ni-bearing minerals of the clay subtype Ni laterite ore (Brand and others, 1998; Freyssinet and others, 2005). Most of

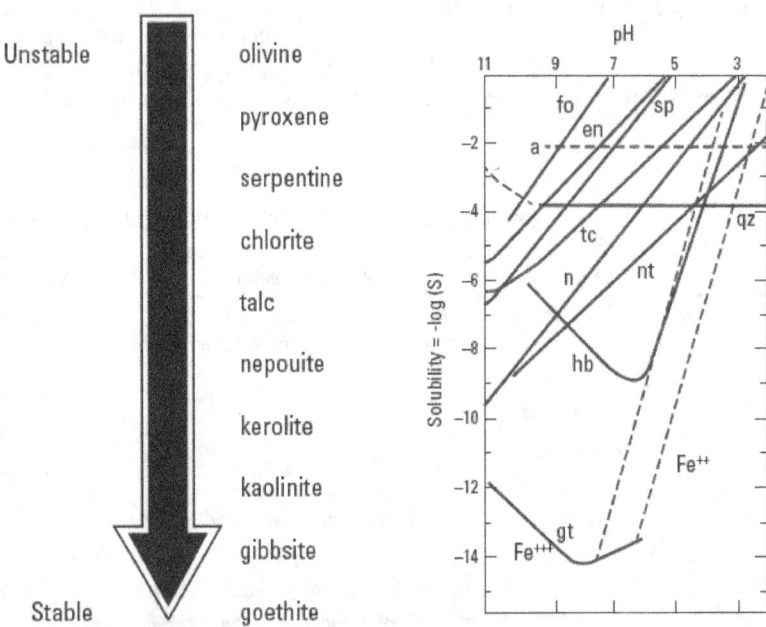

Figure 10. Mineral stability for idealized mineral assemblage found in the progressive weathering of nickel-cobalt laterite deposits, and pH dependence on mineral stability that reflects the mineral progression in a laterite profile. Modified from Golightly (1981, 2010). (fo, forsterite; en, enstatite; sp, serpentine; tc, talc; qz, quartz; a, amorphous silica; gt, goethite; n, nickel serpentine; nt, nickel talc; hb, hornblende; Fe, iron)

the Co is present in the Mn-oxyhydroxides (Brand and others, 1998; Freyssinet and others, 2005). In clay subtype deposits, such as Murrin Murrin, Ni is present mostly in the Fe(III)-rich variety of nontronite, with minor Mg-Fe- and Fe-rich montmorillonite and saponite Ni-bearing clays (Elias, 2006). Manganese-oxides host most of the Co at the top of the clay zone above the transition between the clay and oxide horizons of the laterite profile. Magnetite-maghemite, chlorite, goethite, and opaline silica are the gangue minerals in the clay-rich smectite zone of the profile at Murrin Murrin (Elias, 2006).

Mineral Assemblages, Paragenesis, and Zoning Patterns

A major decrease in Mg content and a drastic shift in mineralogy marks the transition between the saprolite and limonite horizons (Mg discontinuity; Brand and others, 1996; Elias, 2006). The Mg content of the ore horizon has a substantial effect on ore processing, as discussed below. The texture and structure of the minerals become progressively disordered and amorphous upward from the bedrock, through the saprolite and transition zone, and into the limonite and ferricrete caprock. In the saprolite, the structure and fabric of the primary weathered minerals can still be seen, and the volume of the protolith is preserved (isovolumetric weathering). The lower zone of the limonite, which is sometimes referred to as the ferruginous saprolite or saprolite fine, can have some textures of the protolith preserved. It also hosts much of the asbolane growths and accumulations. The upper layer has no preserved protolith texture, and asbolane is absent, unless there are quartz veins cutting the protolith; because of the resilient nature of quartz, this texture can be preserved. Therefore, at the base of the weathering profile, replacement of the parent minerals is isovolumetric. As the weathering advances up the profile, the replacement of chemistry, structure, and texture becomes absolute such that there is no remnant of parent rock mineralogy, texture, or structure.

The oxide minerals are goethite, hematite, asbolane, lithiophorite, and heterogenite. Generally, to the naked eye, the oxide zone appears to be a matrix of Fe-oxyhydroxides, which vary in size and crystalline habit, suggesting several crystallization events, with clumps of black Mn-oxyhydroxides (Roqué-Rosell and others, 2010). In oxide subtype deposits, the limonite horizon also hosts local veins of Mn-oxyhydroxide minerals that contain most of the Co concentration (Elias, 2006). Gangue minerals in the limonite horizon include opaline quartz and some hematite, with minor clays such as nontronite, montmorillonite, and kaolinite (Elias, 2006).

In general, the Mn-oxides and oxyhydroxides are cryptomelane, heterogenite, asbolane, lithiophorite, and minerals with intermediate compositions between asbolane and lithiophorite. These minerals occur with supergene Si as aggregates forming blue-black tufts, as well as lining joints, cracks, root casts, faults, and fissures, forming as replacements of Si minerals serpentine, pyroxene, and olivine, rather than primary formed minerals (Llorca, 1993). Typically, the Co content in the profile increases from the fresh protolith into the transition zone then decreases, commonly suddenly at a Mn discontinuity, similar to Mg at the top of the saprolite. It decreases farther upward towards the ferricrete to a Co content less than that of the protolith, with the ferricrete, Fe cap being barren (Llorca, 1993). Cobalt is enriched in the lower limonite zone in hydrous Mg-silicate subtype deposits, such as Goro, New Caledonia; in oxide subtype deposits, such as Cawse, Western Australia; and in the transition between the lower limonite and the clay zone in clay subtype deposits, such as Murrin Murrin, Western Australia (Llorca, 1993; Elias, 2006).

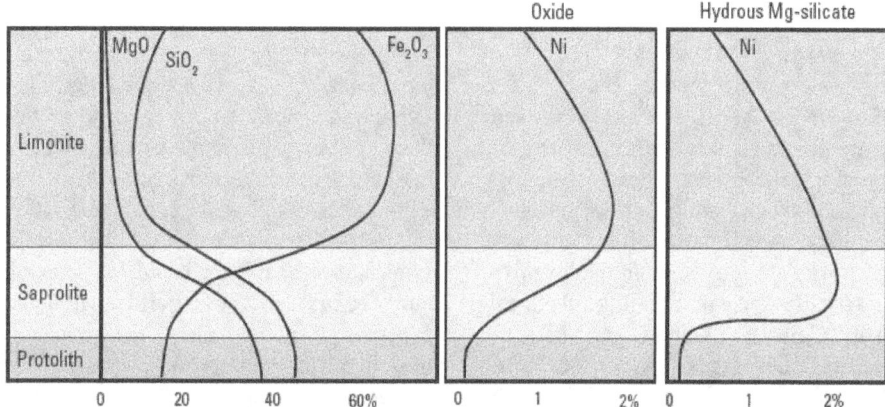

Figure 11. Chemical profile through oxide and hydrous magnesium-silicate subtype nickel-cobalt laterite deposits illustrating the loss of magnesium (Mg) and silicon (Si) along with the concentration of nickel (Ni) and iron (Fe) as the weathering profile develops from the protolith to the limonite. Modified from Schellmann (1971). (%, percent)

The mineralogy of the ore and gangue minerals depends on the mineralogy of the parent rock and hydrology of the weathering profile. For example, in Australia, clay subtype deposits form over Al-bearing orthocumulate peridotites and the spinifex-textured komatiites, whereas the oxide subtype deposits form over mesocumulate and adcumulate dunites that contain little Al (Wells and Butt, 2006; Elias, 2006). All types of Ni-Co laterites generally lack Ni enrichment in hydrous Mg-silicate minerals in their saprolite horizon that formed in a stable tectonic environment with relatively poor drainage, in contrast to those more commonly found in tectonically active, well-drained terrain, such as in New Caledonia (Elias, 2006).

Nickel-cobalt laterite deposits generally exhibit enrichment of Ni toward the center and base of the laterite profile depending on the subtype of deposit. Lower Ni concentrations are present at the top of the limonite zone, increasing through this zone and peaking in the limonite, if it is an oxide subtype; in the clay/transition zone, if it is a clay subtype; and in the saprolite, if it is a hydrous Mg-silicate subtype. The concentration of Ni decreases substantially at the transition between saprolite and fresh protolith (fig. 11). Nickel enrichment in Brazil and in some deposits in South Africa is typically described as different from other laterites. These Ni-Co laterite deposits are generally thin with Ni enrichment towards the top of the profile; weathering occurs in plateaus, and subsequent enrichment in transported deposits forms in lowlands (De Waal, 1971; Trescases and others, 1979; Maynard, 1983). Golightly (2010; written commun., 2011) observed that in some locations in Brazil this may not be the case and that the Ni-Co laterite deposits here are, in fact, in situ deposits. The deposits are relatively thin because the limonite and upper saprolite zones have been eroded in a region of plateau landforms that is typical of the dry-to-wet weathering scenario of laterite development.

Weathering/Supergene Processes

Mineralogical Reactions

Weathering forms Ni-Co laterite deposits. Many factors are involved in creating a complex profile. Weathering depends on the mineralogical characteristics of the parent rock, the redox potential (Eh) and pH of the circulating water, geomorphology, and climate (Ogura, 1986). The Ni-Co laterite deposits are formed from the chemical weathering of ultramafic rocks that removes the most soluble elements (Mg, calcium [Ca], and Si) and concentrates the least soluble elements (Fe, Ni, Mn, Co, Zn, yttrium [Y], Cr, Al, titanium [Ti], zirconium [Zr], and Cu) (Brand and others, 1998). Mechanical weathering of the host material where there are abundant fractures and faults increases the surface area exposed to the water driving the chemical weathering (see the section "Relations to Structures," p. 11).

Olivine, serpentine, enstatite, and chromite weather to residual assemblages of the same minerals, as well as to the secondary minerals listed in table 4. Magnesium, Ca, and silica leach from the parent mineralogy. Iron, Cr, Al, Ti, Zr, and Cu are residually concentrated. Nickel, Mn, Co, Zn, and Y are secondarily enriched (Golightly, 1981).

Rates of Reactions and Controlling Factors

The earlier section "Duration of Mineralizing Processes" on p. 9 provides additional discussion on the rates and factors controlling reactions. Temperature, moisture, and pH can influence the rate of the chemical reactions involved in developing a Ni-Co laterite profile. Temperature can increase the rate of reaction by two or three times with every 10°C (Butt and Zeegers, 1992a). Golightly (Golightly Geoscience, written commun., 2011) argues that temperature is strongly buffered in the rainforest environment to a narrow range and that its main influence, perhaps, is to increase the rate of rainforest growth, rate of oxidation of organic detritus, and supply of soil acids to the weathering process. Water is a key factor in the weathering process. Water acts as a reagent in the hydrolysis of minerals that are unstable at surface conditions, such as olivine. It acts as the leaching agent for the least soluble elements in the profile and as the transporting agent for the elements that residually concentrate as secondary minerals that define the in situ Ni-Co laterite mineralization. Water is also the mechanism for the transport of primary Ni-Co laterite that is later reconcentrated in transported deposits (Butt and Zeegers, 1992a; Golightly, 1981).

Effects of Micro- and Macro-Climates

Temperature and precipitation are key factors in the weathering process. A higher mean soil temperature can increase the kinetics of the weathering process (Butt and Zeegers, 1992a; Elias, 2002). The amount of water available to run through the soil profile determines the amount of weathering that will take place—the more water available, the faster the weathering process, and the longer the exposure to percolating water, the better. A tropical to subtropical climate, where there is a period of intense chemical weathering, allows for the dissolution of metals moving towards saturation, followed by a dry period allowing for precipitation (de Vletter, 1978).

Most areas hosting Ni-Co laterite deposits experienced a tropical to subtropical climate, but some of these may currently be in an arid or semiarid environment. They have each experienced enough rainfall and sufficiently warm temperatures in the past to allow for pervasive chemical weathering (Gleeson and others, 2003). Those deposits that lie in areas of currently arid climate, such as deposits in Australia, the United States, and Europe, are remnants of early, more humid climates (Brand and others, 1998). Tropical, savanna, subtropical, or humid-to-warm Mediterranean climates have produced Ni-Co laterite deposits, although savanna climates are considered to be the most productive (Freyssinet and others, 2005). The Golightly (1981, 2010) classification of deposits as wet, dry-to-wet, and wet-to-dry focuses on the development of the deposits on the basis of their climate history.

Effects of Hydrologic Setting

The effects of poorly drained and well-drained soil profiles have been discussed throughout this model. The subtypes of the Ni-Co laterite deposit are closely tied to the drainage or lack thereof in the weathering profile. Well-drained profiles generally have higher concentrations of Ni in the saprolite horizon in hydrous Mg-silicate minerals, whereas poorly drained profiles are more likely to have Ni enrichment in clays or Fe-oxides depending on the parent material. The Al-rich parent rocks yield clay subtype deposits, whereas Al-poor parent rocks produce oxide or siliceous oxide subtype deposits (Golightly, 1981; Elias, 2006). Supergene enrichment of Ni will not take place if the water table lies within the limonite zone because Ni released into solution will be dispersed laterally rather than be trapped in a drained saprolite zone (Golightly, 2010). The topographic setting of Ni-Co laterite deposits can be attributed to drainage. For example, hydrous Mg-silicate subtype deposits that form in well-drained, tectonically active regions are present on hills, ridges, and plateau edges. Lack of drainage increases the deposition of silica in a weathered profile. In regions where poorly drained profiles are now exposed, such as is characteristic of some deposits in Brazil, peneplain remnants form highlands where, because of the amount of Si in their profile, the Ni-Co laterite mineralization is preserved (Golightly, 2010).

Geochemical Characteristics

Trace Element, Element Association, and Zoning Pattern

The Ni-Co laterites consist mostly of anomalous Si, Fe, Mg, Mn, Ni, and Co, with minor Al, Ca, and Cr enrichments (table 5; Golightly, 1981; Maynard, 1983). Trace elements used for exploration for Ni-Co laterite deposits are mainly Ni and Co themselves (see below). The laterite profile is essentially a zoned pattern of mineralogy, texture, and structure such that, depending on the conditions of formation, one of the three subtypes of Ni-Co laterite deposits form.

On a deposit scale, along with high concentrations of Ni and Co, an understanding of the content of Mg, Fe, and Si in the ore horizon is critical for economic ore processing. The content of Mg, Fe, and Si determines what ore processing can be implemented. General chemistry of some hydrous Mg-silicate and clay subtype laterite profiles are listed in table 5. Evans and others (1979), Gleeson and others (2003), Imrie and Lane (2004), and Golightly (2010) provide more data on the average concentration of these elements. Typically,

hydrous Mg-silicate subtype ore contains too high a concentration of MgO to be suitable for HPAL treatment (Dalvi and others, 2004).

Stable Isotope Geochemistry

Gaudin and others (2005) determined concentrations of isotopes of oxygen ($\delta^{18}O$) and hydrogen (δD) of smectite from the Murrin Murrin deposit in Australia. They noted the smectite has a light stable isotopic signature typical of weathering clays ($\delta^{18}O$ of 20.3 to 24.3 per mil (‰) and δD of –98 to –60‰). This indicates the smectite formed from low-temperature, meteoric water-rock interactions.

Radiogenic Isotope Geochemistry

There are no direct radiogenic isotope dates of Ni-Co laterite deposits (Freyssinet and others, 2005). Aeromagnetic data and isotope measurements of the radiation defects in clays have been applied to narrow down periods of laterite formation (Batista and others, 2008; Retallack, 2010). However, recent work by Shuster and others (2005) and Heim and others (2006) has shown that (U-Th)/helium (He) dating of goethite is a robust new application of this isotope system for weathering geochronology.

Retallack (2010) summarized $^{40}Ar/^{39}Ar$ and K-Ar age dating of Mn-oxide minerals from papers by Vasconcelos and others (1994), Li and Vasconcelos (2002), and Beauvais and others (2008). He notes the argon isotope ages reported on a few Mn-rich laterites represented the timing of weathering in the laterite profiles, and this can demonstrate that there are periods more favorable for laterite formation than others. With Mn-oxides occurring in many Ni-Co laterites, the application of (U-Th)/He geochronology of goethite and the development of dating techniques that can treat single grains (Thiry and others, 1999) provide new potential for future absolute dating of Ni-Co laterite profiles.

Petrology of Associated Igneous Rocks

The mineral constituents of the protolith determine its vulnerability to weathering and define the elements available for leaching and (or) concentration; the crystal texture and shape provide structure through which weathering occurs (Elias, 2002). The dominant minerals in metamorphosed ultramafic igneous rocks are olivine and serpentine, which are both highly susceptible to chemical weathering (Elias, 2002). Minor minerals are pyroxene, chromite, and chlorite. Serpentinization of ultramafic rocks occurs at relatively shallow depths with a great quantity of water and temperatures not exceeding 450°C; this process results in a substantial increase in porosity because of the increase in bulk volume (Burger, 1996). The serpentinization of olivine benefits the development of Ni-Co laterite in several ways. Serpentine

Table 5. Bulk chemistry from the hydrous magnesium-silicate and clay subtype nickel-cobalt laterite profiles at the Bonsora Soroako deposit, Indonesia, and the Brogla deposit, Queensland, Australia. Data from Arancibia (1975) and Golightly (1981, 2010).

[m, meter]

Sample no.	Sample description	Depth (m)	Fe	FeO	Fe	Co	Al	TiO	MgO	SiO	CaO	K₂O	Cr₂O₃	MnO	Ni	Co
	Brolga, Queensland, Australia															
2.5	Pisolite	0.8	41.50		59.34	0.02	-	-		14.10	-	-	-	0.22	0.223	0.02
5	Pisolite	1.7	44.00		62.91	0.013	-	-		11.70	-	-	-	0.14	0.17	0.013
8	Pisolite	2.7	41.00		58.62	0.019	-	-		14.30	-	-	-	0.18	0.26	0.019
12.5	Pisolite	4.2	41.13		58.81	0.012	-	-		14.90	-	-	-	0.1	0.25	0.012
16	Pisolite	5.3	41.13		58.81	0.028	-	-		13.30	-	-	-	0.22	0.335	0.028
18	Pisolite	6.0	43.45		62.12	0.051	-	-		11.60	-	-	-	0.39	0.48	0.051
20	Pisolite	6.7	44.03		62.95	0.033	-	-		11.20	-	-	-	0.28	0.438	0.033
10	Pisolite	3.3	41.50		59.34	0.015	-	-	1.20	14.90	-	-	-	0.16	0.223	0.015
22.5	Nontronite	7.5	36.27		51.86	0.033	-	-	2.60	26.00	-	-	-	0.29	0.843	0.033
25	Nontronite	8.3	30.40		43.47	0.023	-	-	4.00	41.00	-	-	-	0.13	1.123	0.023
37.5	Nontronite	12.5	28.73		41.08	0.283	-	-	4.40	39.60	-	-	-	1.07	1.66	0.283
40	Nontronite	13.3	28.33		40.51	0.224	-	-	4.40	38.60	-	-	-	0.96	1.6	0.224
42.5	Nontronite	14.2	28.23		40.36	0.179	-	-	4.40	38.80	-	-	-	0.8	1.613	0.179
30	Nontronite	10.0	26.57		37.99	0.216	-	-	4.40	43.20	-	-	-	0.99	1.607	0.216
27.5	Nontronite	9.2	27.10		38.75	0.051	-	-	4.60	45.20	-	-	-	0.31	1.203	0.051
32.5	Nontronite	10.8	26.43		37.79	0.348	-	-	4.60	42.30	-	-	-	1.35	1.78	0.348
35	Nontronite	11.7	26.20		37.46	0.341	-	-	4.70	42.20	-	-	-	1.23	1.807	0.341
45	Nontronite	15.0	27.37		39.13	0.177	-	-	5.10	41.20	-	-	-	0.96	1.83	0.177
47.5	Nontronite	15.8	25.00		35.74	0.136	-	-	6.00	47.90	-	-	-	0.75	2	0.136
50	Serpentine saprolite	16.7	21.23		30.35	0.081	-	-	6.80	48.40	-	-	-	0.46	1.96	0.081
52.5	Serpentine saprolite	17.5	28.43		40.65	0.059	-	-	8.00	49.10	-	-	-	0.42	1.813	0.059
55	Serpentine saprolite	18.3	21.20		30.31	0.057	-	-	12.60	48.60	-	-	-	0.45	1.81	0.057
57.5	Serpentine saprolite	19.2	15.83		22.63	0.03	-	-	19.80	48.30	-	-	-	0.31	1.403	0.03
60	Serpentine saprolite	20.0	15.90		22.73	0.045	-	-	19.90	48.50	-	-	-	0.37	1.503	0.045
62.5	Serpentine saprolite	20.8	12.93		18.49	0.029	-	-	22.80	49.20	-	-	-	0.29	1.26	0.029
65	Serpentine saprolite	21.7	11.40		16.30	0.02	-	-	24.60	47.10	-	-	-	0.23	0.833	0.02
70	Serpentine saprolite	23.3	11.28		16.13	0.024	-	-	25.80	49.70	-	-	-	0.24	0.565	0.024
67.5	Serpentine saprolite	22.5	10.30		14.73	0.022	-	-	32.70	48.50	-	-	-	0.19	0.595	0.022

Table 5. Bulk chemistry from the hydrous magnesium-silicate and clay subtype nickel-cobalt laterite profiles at the Bonsora Soroako deposit, Indonesia, and the Brogla deposit, Queensland, Australia. Data from Arancibia (1975) and Golightly (1981, 2010).—Continued

[m, meter]

Sample no.	Sample description	Depth (m)	Fe	FeO	Fe	Co	Al	TiO	MgO	SiO	CaO	K₂O	Cr₂O₃	MnO	Ni	Co
									Bonsora Soroako, Indonesia							
C 1-2	Limonite	2	45.08	0.00	64.45	0.092	7.30	0.18	4.10	6.50	0.11	0.00	3.12	0.60	1.12	0.092
C 3-4	Limonite	3.5	46.58	0.00	66.60	0.088	7.70	0.12	3.05	4.55	0.11	0.00	3.18	0.90	1.10	0.088
C 5-6	Limonite	5.5	46.86	0.00	67.00	0.154	7.50	0.13	2.75	4.85	0.16	0.00	2.86	1.18	1.27	0.154
C 7-8	Limonite	7.5	40.19	0.00	58.50	0.149	4.80	0.09	6.45	12.65	0.12	0.04	2.58	0.97	1.82	0.149
C 9-10	Serpentine saprolite	9.5	19.72	0.17	28.20	0.073	2.25	0.07	21.25	29.30	0.13	0.02	1.44	0.42	2.67	0.073
C 11-12	Serpentine saprolite	11.5	27.07	0.81	38.70	0.048	3.45	0.08	16.00	23.90	0.12	0.03	0.88	0.24	1.85	0.048
C 13-14	Serpentine saprolite	13.5	13.04	0.39	18.65	0.018	1.48	0.06	28.15	34.65	0.13	0.03	0.88	0.24	1.85	0.018
C 15-16	Serpentine saprolite	15.5	7.76	0.17	11.10	0.019	0.75	0.05	34.85	39.15	0.11	0.03	0.51	0.12	0.50	0.019
C 17-18	Serpentine saprolite	17.5	7.41	0.41	10.60	0.018	1.10	0.06	34.80	39.70	0.25	0.03	0.52	0.15	0.25	0.018
C 19-20	Serpentine saprolite	19.5	6.82	0.39	9.75	0.015	1.10	0.05	35.30	39.45	0.37	0.02	0.48	0.12	0.22	0.015
S220	Boulders	10.5	5.60	0.78	8.00	-	0.80	0.05	32.65	40.00	0.19	0.03	0.47	0.13	3.45	-
S224	Boulders	10.5	7.73	0.65	11.05	-	0.70	0.05	32.00	38.20	0.10	0.03	0.49	0.12	2.70	-
S225	Boulders	10.5	6.54	0.29	9.35	-	0.90	0.06	34.30	38.85	0.12	0.02	0.40	0.10	2.35	-
4 cut	Boulders	13.5	5.57	0.22	7.96	-	0.65	0.05	34.38	39.65	0.11	0.02	0.41	0.10	2.70	-

can be residually enriched in Ni during the supergene ore-forming process, and the structure of the saprolite stems from the microscopic serpentine network developed along crystal surfaces and fractures in the parent rock (fig. 12; Pelletier, 1996). Cumulate texture is prevalent in the komatiite parent rocks. Cumulus olivine crystals are present in a matrix of postcumulus crystals that formed or recrystallized from the intercumulus liquid (fig. 13). The serpentinization and cumulate textures provide the structure and porosity, which allow hydrolysis to occur (figs. 12 and 13).

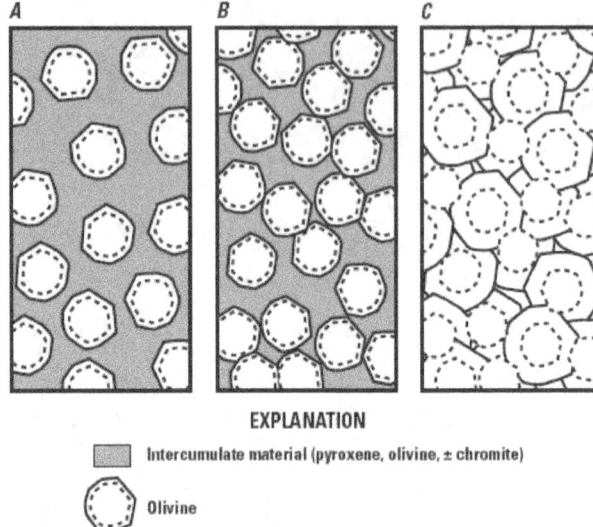

EXPLANATION

Intercumulate material (pyroxene, olivine, ± chromite)

Olivine

Figure 13. Textures of serpentinized cumulate rocks. *A,* Orthocumulate texture. *B,* Mesoculumate texture. *C,* Adcumulate texture. Dotted line shows outer edge of olivine cumulate crystal; the outer rim is crystallized from intercumulate material. Adapted from Raymond (1995).

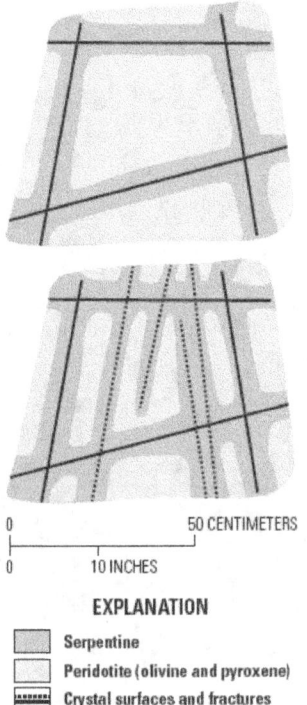

0   50 CENTIMETERS
0   10 INCHES

EXPLANATION

Serpentine
Peridotite (olivine and pyroxene)
Crystal surfaces and fractures

Figure 12. Graphical representation of the enhancement of serpentinization of peridotite around crystal faces and fractures illustrating the expansion of surface area made available to laterite weathering by the prograde metamorphism. Adapted from Pelletier (1996).

Olivine and pyroxene in ultramafic rocks tend to be more Mg-rich than those minerals in mafic and felsic rocks. The key feature of ultramafic lithologies that lend to them being the protoliths to Ni-Co laterite deposits is the instability of their principal mineralogy (fig. 10). Hydrolysis releases Mg, Ca, and Si from olivine and serpentine, which constitute 85–91 percent of the primary-rock material (Samama, 1986). Also critical are an original Ni content between 0.2 and 0.4 wt%, the absence of quartz thus increasing the instability of the rock, and the small amount of insoluble elements resulting in a highly concentrated residuum of stable secondary minerals containing Ni±Co (Golightly, 1981; Alcock, 1988; Elias, 2001, 2002; Gleeson and others, 2003). Australian deposits with Al-bearing protolith tend to form clay subtype deposits (Elias, 2006).

Petrology of Associated Sedimentary Rocks

Sedimentary rocks do not play a role in the genesis of Ni-Co laterite deposits, but in some areas, they provide cover that can preserve the supergene mineralization from complete weathering and erosion. Deposits in Albania and Greece have been preserved under limestone or molasse, which formed in shallow-water environments during epeirogenic cycles of immersion and uplift (Valeton and others, 1987; Eliopoulos and Economou-Eliopoulos, 2000; Panagiotou and Michalako-poulos, 2000). Limestones overlying Ni-Co laterite deposits in Albania generally have a clean contact with weathered horizons (Panagiotou and Michalakopoulos, 2000). Various textures and intercalations of silcrete and chert in many of the weathered profiles in this region give evidence of reworking, transport, redeposition, and metamorphism. In some locations in this region, limestone serves as the deposition surface, or footwall, on which laterite ore was redeposited after transport (Glaskovsky and others, 1977; Eliopoulos and Economou-Eliopoulos, 2000; Freyssinet and others, 2005).

Petrology of Associated Metamorphic Rocks

Preceding Ni-Co laterite formation, the primary hydration or prograde metamorphism of the protolith ultramafic rocks to serpentinite has a substantial effect on the formation of the deposits. The degree of serpentinization affects the type of mineralogy that develops in the laterite weathering process and the geomorphology of the laterite profile and has implications for concentrate of ore during mining and crushing. Golightly (1981) deemed the degree of serpentinization to be one of the two key factors in the development of Ni-Co laterite along with drainage.

Residual primary serpentine can be Ni-enriched during weathering because Ni is present in lizardite, the serpentine mineral formed during post-magmatic serpentinization as a substitution for Mg. In a laterite profile developed from a highly serpentinized parent, garnierite is rare, and lizardite is the main ore mineral (Golightly, 1981; Pelletier, 1996; Freyssinet and others, 2005). The subtype of deposit can be influenced by degree of metamorphism. Clay subtype deposits are noted to develop only from serpentinized peridotites (Gleeson and others, 2003; Elias, 2006) because serpentinization contributes to poor drainage that is key in the development of clay-rich ores (Pelletier, 1996; Gleeson and others, 2003). Garnierite is not typically present in Ni-Co laterite deposits developed from pervasively serpentinized ultramafic protoliths (Golightly, 1981). Mineralogy of the weathering profile horizons can be affected by the degree of metamorphism because protoliths of partially serpentinized ultramafic rocks can form smectite in the saprolite horizon where the terrain is poorly drained (Golightly, 1981).

Because serpentine is more resistant than fresh olivine during the lateritic weathering process, saprolite derived from serpentinized rocks exhibits better relative cohesion (Orloff, 1968; Pelletier, 1996). This stability can have an influence on the thickness, where serpentinized protoliths tend to have thicker saprolite zones because serpentinization develops a microscopic network allowing for deeper penetration of water through the rock compared to the fresher parent lithology (Orloff, 1968; Pelletier, 1996; Gleeson and others, 2003). Troly and others (1979) claimed that parent rock with 0–10 percent primary serpentinization relies more on mineral cleavage than fractures to determine the pervasiveness of weathering because the distance between fractures is 10 times less than a protolith with 70–95 percent serpentinization.

In regions where pyroxene in the parent rock has been metamorphosed to clinochlore, as in Brazil, the chlorite is replaced by nickeliferous vermiculite during weathering and laterite formation (Brindley and de Souza 1975 a, b; Barros de Oliveira and others, 1992).

In Ni-Co laterite deposits developed from unserpentinized ultramafic rocks, ore in the saprolite zone of the weathering profile develops as weathering rims surrounding fragments of fresh parent rock with a matrix of garnierite and quartz veining. This ore can be upgraded before processing by crushing and separating the barren unserpentinized rock cores (Golightly, 1981).

Theory of Deposit Formation

Ore Deposit System Affiliations

The Ni-Co laterite deposits are affiliated by process with bauxite and Au-, Fe-, Nb- and phosphate-bearing laterite deposits (Freyssinet and others, 2005).

Sources of Nickel and Cobalt

The Ni-Co laterites are supergene deposits that form from pervasive chemical and mechanical weathering of ultramafic rocks. These ultramafic rocks hold 0.2–0.4 percent Ni within olivine or serpentine. It is present, but less abundant, in accessory pyroxene and chromite.

Sources of Fluids Involved in Ore Component Transport and Character of Conduits/Pathways that Focus Ore Forming Fluids

The water responsible for this process is circulating rain water and water within the water table. Nickel re-precipitation occurs upon saturation; it is deposited with the hydrated alteration minerals rather than remaining dissolved in the solution leaching the Mg and Si. The percolating water travels the path of least resistance, relying on protolith crystal structure and inherited structure, cracks, fissures, and faults.

Chemical Transport and Transfer Processes

The process of ore formation is the hydrolysis and oxidation of Ni- and Co-bearing minerals and the progressive weathering of the Fe-oxyhydroxides and clays that form in this process. This process includes leaching the most soluble elements (Mg and Si) from the parent material and residually concentrating the least soluble elements (Fe, Ni, and Co). Olivine is weathered to an amorphous ferric-silicic gel, smectite, or quartz; serpentine is partially dissolved and re-precipitated with goethite.

Supergene Enrichment Processes

The enrichment of Ni is controlled within the mineralogy of the profile relative to Mg by the hierarchy of mineral solubilities shown in figure 10. Dissolved Mg, Ni, and Si may be precipitated as colloform crusts of the amorphous garnierite minerals, serpentine-nepouite, kerolite-pimelite, sepiolite-falcondoite, and quartz in open fractures and open breccia matrices. Manganese-oxide minerals, such as asbolane, lithiophorite, and cryptomelane, form within fractures and open spaces by the precipitation of the dissolved Mn, Co, and Ni. Smectite minerals or talc replace pyroxene. The secondary silicates are progressively weathered through the top of the saprolite zone until they are entirely depleted. The lower part of the limonite zone consists of Fe-oxide and insoluble chromite, which accumulate with Ni- and Co-bearing Mn-oxides. Mechanical transport and further meteoric water leaching release Ni, Co, and Mn from the upper part of the limonite zone to be re-precipitated at deeper levels in the profile. Finally, at the top of the profile, goethite is oxidized to hematite.

If the profile is well drained, serpentine and pyroxene may not be replaced by smectites, and a hydrous Mg-silicate zone develops. If poorly drained, a smectite clay zone containing Ni-rich nontronite develops. If improperly drained because of too few fractures in the bedrock, little or no hydrous Mg-silicates form. If the water table lies in the lower limonite zone, Ni may be entirely removed from the profile laterally in the groundwater without absolute enrichment of Ni occurring. It is possible that Mn, Co, and Ni may diffuse upwards, precipitating at a redox front in profiles with poor drainage.

Exploration/Resource Assessment Guides

Geological and Geophysical

Several factors interplay to form Ni-Co laterite deposits. On a regional scale, parent-rock lithology and climate history are paramount to determining a permissive tract. A variety of technical and traditional techniques to understand the geology, such as remote sensing, high-resolution geophysical surveying, and ground mapping, can identify ophiolite sequences and komatiites that contain dunite, peridotite, and olivine cumulates with varying degrees of serpentinization. Analysis of aerial photography and satellite imagery for critical geomorphology has led to deposit discoveries (Golightly, 2010). For a region to be prospective, there must be ultramafic rocks with the dominant mineralogy of olivine or the primary alteration phase, serpentine, which have had exposure to pervasive weathering. Developing an understanding of regional paleoclimate to place these identified ultramafic rocks in a suitable environment for at least one million years of their history is required to identify undiscovered Ni-Co laterite deposits.

Geochemical

Stream sediment and soil geochemistry have aided in the discovery of Ni-Co laterites, such as in Cote d'Ivoire, Cameroon, Burundi, and Brazil (Golightly, 2010). The Ni-Co laterite deposits have a geochemical signature of Fe, Mg, Ni, and Cr, less consistently Mn and Co, and rarely Cu, Zn, and PGEs (Lelong and others, 1976; Derkmann and Jung, 1986; Alcock, 1988; Butt and Zeegers, 1992b; Brand and others, 1998; Cornelius and others, 2001; Golightly, 2010). They commonly lack the PGE and Cu enrichments that are a common indication of the lateritic weathering of Ni-sulfide deposits. Australian companies discovered Ni-Co laterite deposits, such as Murrin Murrin, while exploring for Ni-sulfide deposits. When drilling Ni and Co anomalies, Ni-Co laterite deposits were discovered laying over cumulates rather than a Ni-sulfide deposit (Wells, 2003; Butt, 2009).

Attributes Required for Inclusion in Permissive Tract at Various Scales

The history of discovery and exploitation of Ni-Co laterites, in general, initially focused on tectonically active regions as areas of supergene enrichment of Ni and Co from obducted sheets of ophiolite or Alpine-type ophiolites, such as those in New Caledonia, Cuba, the United States, and southern Europe. More recently, Ni-Co laterites have been discovered and exploited in tectonically stable cratonic environments in Australia and Brazil. Understanding the tectonic history of ultramafic rocks exposed to pervasive weathering can open new possibilities for prospective areas.

Knowledge that Enables Favorability Zonation of Permissive Tracts

In an area that has permissive geology and a favorable climate or paleoclimate, an understanding of modes of preservation of these supergene deposits is essential. Understanding the keys to Ni-Co enrichment, such as drainage and a cyclical dry season giving the profile the time and opportunity to develop into a more enriched laterite profile, are essential. An understanding of past and present climates in an area is necessary. For example, the Australian deposits are preserved not only because they are in a stable craton, but also because they transitioned into a dry climate, preventing further leaching and erosion of the Ni-Co mineralization developed in a wetter past. The deposits in Riddle, Oregon, have been preserved because the area has transitioned from a subtropical or humid-to-warm Mediterranean climate to a comparatively less tropical climate in the present day. Other deposits, such as those in Albania and Greece, formed in the Jurassic and were buried in the Cretaceous, preserving them for present-day exploitation.

Geoenvironmental Features and Anthropogenic Mining Effects

Pre-Mining Baseline Signatures in Soil, Sediment, and Water

Mine permitting and remediation require an estimate of pre-mining natural background conditions to serve as a goal for post-mining reclamation. Complete baseline characterization studies for Ni-Co laterites are limited in the literature, particularly in regard to the widespread climatic settings in which they are found. Baseline data are available in the literature for soil and stream sediment from a variety of deposits. Within and adjacent to the lateritic profile, soil and stream sediments may contain anomalous abundances of Ni, Fe, Co, Al, and Cr and possibly Mn, Pb, Zn, and PGEs (Golightly, 1979b, 1981; Bowles, 1986; Butt and others, 1992; Grey and others, 1996). Soil development depends mainly on the lithology of the parent material and slope stability. Typically, as in the Loma Ortega Ni-laterite deposit, Dominican Republic, Ni concentrations strongly increase upward from the peridotite protolith through to the saprolite and then sharply decrease in the ferruginous saprolite (Gallardo and others, 2010). Nickel is highly enriched in the saprolite zone and may be as great as 3.16 NiO wt%. The soils are generally nutrient poor.

Groundwater and surface-water baseline geochemical data from these deposit areas are sparse in the literature. Therefore, extrapolation of the insights provided by the case studies summarized herein to other deposits should be done with caution. However, groundwater samples collected in the Sukinda valley, Orissa, India, upstream and away from the mining area, contain low total dissolved solids (TDS) ranging from 50–507 milligrams per liter (mg/L). These water samples were nearly neutral to mildly alkaline (pH 6.1–7.6). The electrical conductivity of these samples varied from low to moderate (300–750 microsiemens per centimeter [μS/cm]) for a post-monsoon period, whereas it was somewhat less for a pre-monsoon period (50–490 μS/cm) (Dhakate and Singh, 2008). The electrical conductivity and pH of this water are within the permissible limits of potable water (World Health Organization, 1993). The concentrations of total suspended solids (TSS) of 12–64 mg/L for the post-monsoon period and 4–35 mg/L for the pre-monsoon period are indistinguishable from water draining the mined Ni laterite. The permissible limit of TSS in potable water is only 10 mg/L (World Health Organization, 1993). The Cr(VI) concentration varies from 0.001 to 0.018 mg/L in dug wells and bore wells upstream from the mined area. Values for Fe and Cu ranged from 0.18 to 0.34 mg/L and 0.02 to 0.183 mg/L, respectively.

Surface-water concentrations for Cr(VI) range from 0.03 to 0.07 mg/L from the upstream reaches of the Damsal Nala River that run through the mining area. Ni values were not reported for the waters, although the area is considered one of the richest chromite- and Ni-producing areas and supplies 90 percent of India's demand (Rao and others, 2003).

Similar pH values are reported from mine and local groundwater geochemical surveys at and near the Cerro Matoso deposit, Colombia (6.5–8.1; Gleeson and others, 2003), and 16 sites in New Caledonia (5.5–8.3; Trescases, 1975) (table 6). The chemistry of the water from these two studies reveals the process of the weathering of the profile more than it provides a clear indication of background levels from an environmental impact perspective. It illustrates the removal of Mg and Si from the profile and indicates that major complexing anions are probably carbonate, bicarbonate, and organic acids because the chloride and sulfate levels are relatively low, <150 ppm (table 6). Although Ni, Fe, Mn, and Co were detected in analyses of surface water, spring, and well samples, the average values (Ni = 0.30 parts per million [ppm], Fe = 1.16 ppm, Mn = 0.13 ppm, Co = 0.30 ppm) suggest the elements are relatively immobile in waters draining the developed lateritic profiles.

Past and Future Mining Methods, Ore Treatment, and Footprint

Nickel laterites generally are mined via open-pit methods, although some deposits in Greece have been exploited underground. A variety of process routes are used to extract Ni from the ore. Hydrometallurgical processes include HPAL and heap leach, both of which generally are followed by solvent extraction–electrowinning (SX-EW) for recovery of Ni. Another hydrometallurgical option is the Caron process, which consists of roasting followed by ammonia leaching and precipitation as Ni carbonate. Most commonly, pyrometallurgical processes, such as ferronickel and matte or high carbon ferronickel smelting, are used (see Dalvi and others, 2004, table 2). The dominant Ni mineralogy has a substantial influence on what ore process is used: HPAL and Caron processes work well for oxide subtype ores; HPAL and smelting are effective for clay subtype ores; and pyrometallurgical processes are most appropriate for hydrous Mg-type ores, although they do not allow for the extraction of Co (Dalvi and others, 2004). Current Ni-Co laterite processing methods are summarized in table 7.

Most Ni-Co laterite deposits have at least some uneconomic overburden, which needs to be considered in mine planning. Either permanent or temporary storage of the uneconomic material needs to be established.

Historically, most Ni-Co production has been derived from sulfide ores; laterite ores provided only a modest source. Worldwide, large Co production and reserves are derived from the sedimentary Cu deposits of Congo (Kinshasa) and Zambia. Since the late 1990s, major new Ni-Co laterite projects have been developed using improvements in materials and processing technology, such as HPAL. Therefore, future production is increasingly shifting to laterite ores. With the increasing proportion of more technically and economically viable laterite Ni-Co coming into production, the corresponding associated environmental cost is greater (for example, an increasing footprint from Ni-Co production; Mudd, 2009, 2010). Data compiled by Mudd (2009) from

Table 6. Mine and local groundwater chemistry (in parts per million) from samples collected from the Cerro Matoso S.A. mine and surrounding area, Colombia, and areas throughout New Caledonia. Data from Gleeson and others (2003)

[<, less than]

Location	Setting	pH	HCO$_3$	Cl	SO$_4$	Ca	Na	K	Mg	Si	Fe	Mn	Al	Ni	Co	Cr	Zn	NH$_4$
New Caledonia[1]																		
Kouaoua	Ferricrete water table	5.5	36.6	4.3		0.4	2.5	0.2	0.0	0.0	-	-	-	-	-	-	-	-
Pourina	Ferricrete water table	7.5	18.0	7.8	1.0	0.0	4.3	0.2	0.4	0.1	-	-	-	-	-	-	-	-
Tiébaghi	Ferricrete water table	6.9	8.5	8.5	1.5	0.4	4.4	0.1	1.1	1.7	-	-	-	-	-	-	-	-
Ile des Pins	Base of profile water table	7	32.0	18.5		0.2	9.2	0.3	7.2	5.9	-	-	-	-	-	-	-	-
Kouaoua	Base of profile water table	7.3	41.5	7.1		0.4	2.2	0.2	11.5	1.9	-	-	-	-	-	-	-	-
Bumbéa	Base of profile water table	7.5	50.1	6.0		1.1	3.0	0.1	7.5	5.8	-	-	-	-	-	-	-	-
Bumbéa	Base of profile water table	7.5	50.1	6.0		1.2	3.0	0.1	7.8	5.0	-	-	-	-	-	-	-	-
Bumbéa	Base of profile water table	7.5	50.1	6.0		1.1	3.0	0.1	7.7	5.3	-	-	-	-	-	-	-	-
Bumbéa	Base of profile water table	7.5	50.1	6.0		1.5	3.0	0.1	8.2	3.6	-	-	-	-	-	-	-	-
Bumbéa	High in the water catchment	7.6	67.4	6.7	3.9	0.2	2.7	0.4	13.2	9.3	-	-	-	-	-	-	-	-
Bumbéa	High in the water catchment	7.8	53.8	5.9	3.3	0.2	2.7	0.2	12.3	8.3	-	-	-	-	-	-	-	-
Bumbéa	High in the water catchment	7.8	54.0	6.7	6.8	0.2	2.6	0.2	11.8	7.9	-	-	-	-	-	-	-	-
Bumbéa	High in the water catchment	7.5	56.1	6.2	7.9	0.2	2.7	0.2	12.0	8.0	-	-	-	-	-	-	-	-
Ile des Pins	High in the water catchment	8.3	156.3	27.0		0.3	14.7	0.4	36.2	22.7	-	-	-	-	-	-	-	-
Kouaoua	High in the water catchment	7.1	34.2	7.8		0.2	4.2	0.4	7.7	6.8	-	-	-	-	-	-	-	-
Tiébaghi	High in the water catchment	7.9	449.5	12.6		3.8	7.8	1.2	95.6	5.5	-	-	-	-	-	-	-	-
Dumbea	Springs over piedmont	7.3	72.1	8.5		0.8	3.9	0.2	10.6	7.0	-	-	-	-	-	-	-	-
Dumbea	Springs over piedmont	7.7	66.4	11.1	6.5	0.4	5.1	0.2	13.9	10.1	-	-	-	-	-	-	-	-
Dumbea	Springs over piedmont	6.9	29.2	6.7	2.0	0.3	4.4	0.2	5.7	4.2	-	-	-	-	-	-	-	-
Creek Pernod	Springs and streams on ferricrete	7.5	31.0	10.1	3.4	0.2	4.4	0.2	6.9	4.2	-	-	-	-	-	-	-	-
Creek Pernod	Springs and streams on ferricrete	7.0	29.2	8.5	2.4	0.2	4.5	0.2	6.8	4.1	-	-	-	-	-	-	-	-
Creek Pernod	Springs and streams on ferricrete	7.5	36.0	14.6		0.2	4.0	0.2	8.1	4.6	-	-	-	-	-	-	-	-
Creek Pernod	Springs and streams on ferricrete	7.5	35.8	9.8	2.8	0.1	6.5	0.2	7.7	5.3	-	-	-	-	-	-	-	-
Koué	Springs and streams on ferricrete	7.5	29.3	12.4	3.5	0.1	6.2	0.2	6.7	4.9	-	-	-	-	-	-	-	-
Koué	Springs and streams on ferricrete	7.0	22.5	12.8	3.0	0.1	5.2	0.2	5.5	3.2	-	-	-	-	-	-	-	-
Koué	Springs and streams on ferricrete	7.6	45.6	17.5		0.1	5.4	0.2	10.8	5.6	-	-	-	-	-	-	-	-
Koué	Springs and streams on ferricrete	7.6	41.8	8.3	2.2	0.2	5.6	0.2	8.9	6.9	-	-	-	-	-	-	-	-
Prony	Springs and streams on ferricrete	7.6	41.3	11.7	4.5	0.2	6.1	0.2	9.5	6.3	-	-	-	-	-	-	-	-
Prony	Springs and streams on ferricrete	7.1	42.7	11.2	2.9	0.1	5.9	0.2	9.6	5.9	-	-	-	-	-	-	-	-
Prony	Springs and streams on ferricrete	7.6	46.1	15.7		0.1	5.3	0.2	10.6	5.1	-	-	-	-	-	-	-	-
Prony	Springs and streams on ferricrete	7.3	17.6	8.1	1.7	0.1	6.5	0.2	3.8	2.1	-	-	-	-	-	-	-	-

Table 6. Mine and local groundwater chemistry (in parts per million) from samples collected from the Cerro Matoso S.A. mine and surrounding area, Colombia, and areas throughout New Caledonia. Data from Gleeson and others (2003).—Continued

[<, less than]

Location	Setting	pH	HCO₃	Cl	SO₄	Ca	Na[1]	K	Mg	Si	Fe	Mn	Al	Ni	Co	Cr	Zn	NH₄
New Caledonia[1]																		
Lacs	Shallow groundwater	7.3	15.3	13.3	2.6	0.2	6.3	0.2	3.9	1.9	-	-	-	-	-	-	-	-
Lacs	Shallow groundwater	6.8	13.9	10.8	2.2	0.1	5.8	0.2	3.7	1.6	-	-	-	-	-	-	-	-
Lacs	Shallow groundwater	7.5	19.3	18.8		0.1	6.5	0.3	4.9	2.6	-	-	-	-	-	-	-	-
Lacs	Shallow groundwater	7.5	109.9	5.7	8.9	2.6	3.8	0.2	22.3	13.9	-	-	-	-	-	-	-	-
Dumbea	Shallow groundwater	7.3	134.2	9.7	8.2	3.6	4.3	0.2	21.6	11.9	-	-	-	-	-	-	-	-
Tontouta	Shallow groundwater	7.5	356.4	29.1	2.5	14.6	12.6	0.2	125.0	11.9	-	-	-	-	-	-	-	-
Mé Maoya	Rivers flowing of the the west coast massif	7.7	123.3	4.3			2.9	0.1	27.5	11.8	-	-	-	-	-	-	-	-
Kopéto	Rivers flowing of the the west coast massif	7.6	327.4	19.9		1.5	16.9	0.7	70.4	19.3	-	-	-	-	-	-	-	-
Koniambo	Rivers flowing of the the west coast massif	7.7	130.1	8.1			4.0	0.1	28.5	14.6	-	-	-	-	-	-	-	-
Ouazangou	Rivers flowing of the the west coast massif	7.5	286.3	9.8		0.6	5.6	0.2	58.5	19.9	-	-	-	-	-	-	-	-
Kaala	Rivers flowing of the the west coast massif	8.2	199.2	8.5			5.0	0.2	45.1	15.0	-	-	-	-	-	-	-	-
Tiebaghi	Rivers flowing of the the west coast massif	7.7	166.2	12.4	2.0	0.3	7.7	0.2	37.9	12.5	-	-	-	-	-	-	-	-
Colombia[2]																		
Cerro Matoso S.A.	Mine: spring	7.95	-	1.37	5.10	2.87	0.88	0.15	17.59	10.50	0.92	0.16	<0.1	0.28	0.01	<0.05	0.02	0.02
Cerro Matoso S.A.	Mine: trench	7.75	-	1.75	75.63	9.70	0.73	0.03	19.86	3.10	<0.02	0.03	<0.1	<0.05	0.01	0.23	0.03	<0.05
Cerro Matoso S.A.	Mine: spring	8.11	-	1.35	105.04	16.33	1.43	0.21	33.49	10.10	<0.02	0.02	<0.1	<0.05	0.01	<0.05	<0.01	<0.05
Cerro Matoso S.A.	Mine: trench	7.60	-	1.65	52.35	8.33	1.39	0.28	25.72	13.10	0.19	0.02	<0.1	0.11	0.02	<0.05	0.02	0.28
Cerro Matoso S.A.	Mine: waterfall	8.12	-	1.34	64.67	9.15	2.29	0.14	28.02	9.50	<0.02	0.04	<0.1	0.04	0.01	<0.05	0.03	0.10
Cerro Matoso S.A.	Surface: Ure River	7.20	-	1.13	1.07	6.82	3.43	0.45	3.52	10.70	1.17	0.05	<0.1	<0.05	0.01	<0.05	0.02	0.18
Cerro Matoso S.A.	Surface: Ure River	7.30	-	1.06	0.60	7.69	3.25	0.49	3.76	11.10	0.02	0.04	<0.1	<0.05	0.01	<0.05	0.20	0.13
Cerro Matoso S.A.	Surface: well	6.50	-	1.98	0.47	<0.0005	1.09	0.14	5.83	7.60	<0.02	0.01	<0.1	0.76	0.01	<0.05	0.02	0.07
Cerro Matoso S.A.	Surface: steam	6.63	-	1.67	6.34	2.06	0.96	0.15	5.38	4.30	3.51	0.80	<0.1	0.29	0.04	<0.05	0.02	0.06

[1]Trescases, 1975

[2]Gleeson and others, 2004

Table 7.   Processing methods of nickel laterites.

Processing type	Processing method
Pyrometallurgical processing (ore is melted)	Ferro-nickel
	Nickel-matte
	Nickel pig iron
Hydrometallurgical processing (ore is leached by acid)	Pressure acid leaching (PAL) or high-pressure acid leaching (HPAL)
	Atmospheric leaching (AL)
	Heap leaching
Caron processing (ore is reduced at high temperature then leached)	Combines pyrometallurgical and hydrometallurgical processes

various major Ni-Co mines and producers are displayed on figure 14, showing the type of ore processed, ore grades, and metals produced, as well as unit energy consumption and emissions discharges (carbon dioxide). Mudd (2009) analyzed these data with respect to ore type and other important factors (such as electricity source) and concluded that the production of Ni from laterite ores is clearly more energy intensive than sulfide ores. This greater cost is closely associated with a higher greenhouse intensity where greenhouse costs are also closely linked with electricity supply, such as gas or hydroelectricity.

Volume of Mine Waste and Tailings

Typical Ni-laterite ore deposits are very large-tonnage, low-grade deposits located close to the surface. They are commonly greater than or equal to 18 Mt of mineralized material, with a contained resource of greater than 18,000 tonnes of 1 percent Ni; some examples approach 1 billion tonnes of material. Ore deposits of this type are restricted to the weathering mantle developed above ultramafic rocks. These tend to be tabular, flat, and large in area, covering many square kilometers of the surface of the Earth.

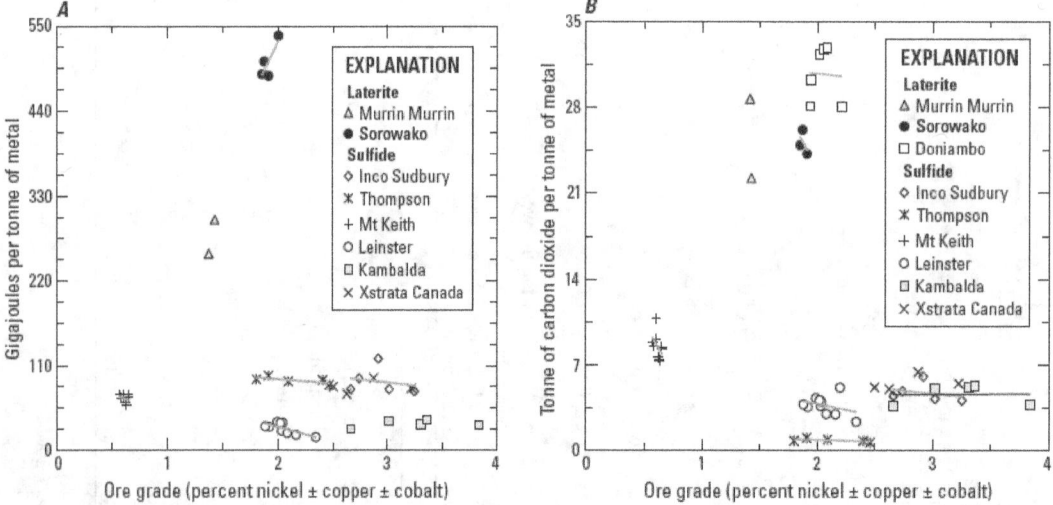

Figure 14.   The relations of ore grade (percent nickel ± copper ± cobalt) and deposit type (laterite and sulfide) to (*A*) unit energy consumption and (*B*) carbon dioxide (CO_2) emission. Approximate linear trend lines are included for some series showing trends of lower and higher use of energy for sulfide and laterite ore processing with higher grade, respectively. Modified from Mudd (2009). (1 kilowatthour = 0.0036 gigajoule)

Mine-Waste Characteristics

Physiochemical Characteristics

The most common ore processing of Ni-Co laterite ores is electric smelting from which the main waste is slag consisting mostly of Fe-oxide, Mg-oxide, and silica, with lesser Ni-oxide, Ti-oxide, Ca-oxide, Cr-oxide, and Al-oxide (Utigard, 1994; den Hoed, 2000; Mu and others, 2010). Other common mine waste produced by acid-leaching methods generally consists of three components: Fe precipitates (the largest fraction), sulfates (gypsum, Mg sulfate), and small quantities of other process sludges. They can be produced as conventional or thickened slurry, paste, or filtered material.

Management options for these materials include (1) conventional tailings impoundments for slurries or paste or (2) in-pit disposal for slurry, paste, or filtered tailings. The resultant slurry or paste will require containment berms similar to those required for ex-pit disposal; filtered residue can be dry stacked in the pit and may require little or no structural containment. Because the waste products contain very high levels of sulfate and Mg and commonly elevated Mn and have a low pH, an environmental containment system, such as a base liner, drains, and closure cap, will be required unless natural geologic containment and suitable climate factors are present (Steemson and Smith, 2009).

Leached Ni-lateritic mine waste has low permeability, which is worsened by re-precipitation of Fe compounds. This increased saturation in the tailings pile results in a vulnerability to liquefaction of the impoundment. High saturation of the material also reduces the ability to support the weight of ground equipment. In addition to having poor slope stability and very poor drainage properties, the residue can be prone to erosion. Nickel laterite residue poses a stark contrast to conventional tailings because it predominantly consists of chemical precipitate of Fe, Mg, and gypsum instead of ground rock with interstitial traces of chemical residue.

Pit Lakes

Studies of pit lakes associated with lateritic Ni-Co deposits are lacking.

Human-Health Issues

Contaminated groundwater plumes associated with tailings impoundments may pose threats to drinking-water supplies, depending on hydrologic and geologic setting and engineering aspects of the mine and the waste piles. Rocks with higher neutralization potentials, such as carbonate rocks, tend to limit the mobility of metals and related compounds. Nickel-cobalt laterite deposits buried by limestone may have this neutralizing advantage. Hydrologic and climatic settings that experience net evaporative loss of water may cause evaporative concentration of solutes that enter groundwater used as drinking-water supplies near mines and waste piles. Improperly constructed water-containment structures may allow contaminated mine water to enter surrounding groundwater. Elements or compounds with the greatest likelihood of contaminating aquatic ecosystems and drinking-water sources for terrestrial organisms include, in alphabetical order, Al, Co, Cu, Cr, Fe, Mn, Ni, sulfate, and Zn.

Climate Effects on Geoenvironmental Signatures

Present climate controls the active weathering on a Ni-Co laterite profile; however, when relief is greatly increased, mechanical erosion is more influential on the elemental dispersion process than climate conditions (Butt, 2009). As mentioned above, temperature and precipitation are critical factors in the development of Ni-Co laterite. Warming of the Earth's atmosphere is thought to (1) increase the amount of water vapor carried by the atmosphere, resulting in increased precipitation and humidity, and (2) increase the mean surface (soil) temperatures. In some areas, such as the southwestern United States, heavy rainfall-drought cycles may become more enhanced end-member patterns. The overall effect would be an increase in the kinetics of the weathering process and a possible increase in areas where lateritic horizons are developing. An additional factor of a cycle of increased rainfall (and rainfall intensity) and drought is a change (presumable increase) in erosion of existing primary Ni-Co laterite deposits. Because of increased incision, down-cutting, and removal of soil, these deposits could potentially be greatly modified, dispersed into non-economic regions, or reconcentrated as transported deposits.

When dealing with laterite processing as in a heap-leach operation, climate consideration is critical in managing safe water flow through a system. Steemson and Smith (2009) argue that the high levels of Mn and Mg dispersion in laterite processing can possibly be controlled in a dry climate with the use of evaporation ponds but not in a wet climate, where drainage from tailings needs to be completely contained or discharged at regulated levels into the ocean.

As noted above, saturation features of the tailings greatly enhance the risk of liquefaction and physical degradation of the tailings impoundment. Given that most Ni-Co laterites are found in tropical or subtropical climates characterized by very high annual precipitation and intense peak storm events, careful monitoring and the application of a temporary geomembrane cover to divert water around the residual pile is necessary.

Acknowledgments

The authors would like to thank Nick Elias and Paul Golightly for providing constructive comments on an earlier version of the manuscript. Editorial efforts by Richard Goldfarb, Kim Otto, and Melanie Parker are greatly appreciated. Reference support by Bridgette Pena was essential for the completion of this manuscript. A big heartfelt thank you is given to the USGS Library staff, especially Alfredo Pinto, for tracking down many obscure references.

References Cited

Alcock, R.A., 1988, The character and occurrence of primary resources available to the nickel industry, *in* Tyroler, G.P., and Landolt, C.A., eds., Extractive metallurgy of nickel and cobalt—Symposium on Metallurgy of Nickel and Cobalt, Phoenix, Ariz., January 25–28, 1988, Proceedings: Warrendale, Pa., Metallurgical Society, p. 67–89.

Arancibia Ramos, O.N., 1975, Mineralogy and chemistry of two nickeliferous laterite soil profiles, Soroako, Sulawesi, Indonesia: Kingston, Canada, Queen's University, Master's thesis, 199 p.

Barros de Oliveira, S.M., Trescases, J.J., and José Melfi, A.J., 1992, Lateritic nickel deposits of Brazil: Mineralium Deposita, v. 27, p. 137–146.

Basile, Andrew, Hughes, Jeffrey, McFarlane, A.J., and Bhargava, S.K., 2010, Development of a model for serpentine quantification in nickel laterite minerals by infrared spectroscopy: Minerals Engineering, v. 23, no. 5, p. 407–412.

Batista, J.A., Blanco, J., and Pérez-Flores, M.A., 2008, Geological interpretation of eastern Cuba laterites from an airborne magnetic and radioactive isotope survey: Geofísica Internacional, v. 47, no. 2, p. 99–113.

Batista-Rodríguez, J.A., 2006, A magnetic survey of mineral resources in northeastern Cuba: Geofísica Internacional, v. 45, no. 1, p. 39–61.

Batista-Rodríguez, J.A., Pérez-Flores, M.A., Quiroga-Goode, G., and Gallardo, L.A., 2007, Geometry of ophiolites in eastern Cuba from 3D inversion of aeromagnetic data, constrained by surface geology: Geophysics, v. 72, no. 3, p. B81–B91.

Beaton, D.W., Kryski, K.M., and Srivastava, R.M., 2011, 43-101 Technical report on the central Moa nickel laterite operation in Eastern Cuba: Prepared for Sherritt International Corporation, accessed June 25, 2012, at *http:// www.sedar.com/GetFile.do?lang=EN&docClass=24 &issuerNo=00002460&fileName=/csfsprod/data123/ filings/01811517/00000001/z%3A%5Crarcher%5C12941- 2081%5CTechRpts%5CMoa.PDF.*

Beauvais, Anicet, Ruffet, Gilles, Hénocque, Olivier, and Colin, Fabrice, 2008, Chemical and physical erosion rhythms of the West African Cenozoic morphogenesis—The ^{39}Ar-^{40}Ar dating of supergene K-Mn oxides: Journal of Geophysical Research—Earth Surface, v. 113, F04007, 15 p. (Also available at *http://dx.doi.org/10.1029/2008JF000996.*)

Berger, V.I., Singer, D.A., Bliss, J.D., and Moring, B.C., 2011, Ni-Co laterite deposits of the world—Database and grade and tonnage models: U.S. Geological Survey Open-File Report 2011–1058, 26 p. (Also available at *http://pubs.usgs. gov/of/2011/1058/.*)

Besairie, H., Bussiére, P., and Randrianarivony, 1961, Reconnaissance des gisements de fer-nickel d'Ambatovy et d'Analamy: Rapport Annuel du Service Geologique [Madagascar], p. 57–72.

Boulangé, Bruno, 1984, Les formation bauxitiques latéritiques de Côte-d'Ivoire—Les faciès, leur distribution et l'évolution du modelé: Mémoir ORSTOM, no. 175, 363 p.

Bowles, J.F.W., 1986, The development of platinum-group minerals in laterites: Economic Geology, v. 81, p. 1278–1285.

Brand, N.W., Butt, C.R.M., and Elias, M., 1998, Nickel laterites—Classification and features: AGSO Journal of Australian Geology and Geophysics, v. 17, p. 81–88.

Brand, N.W., Butt, C.R.M., and Hellsten, K.J., 1996, Structural and lithological controls in the formation of the Cawse nickel laterite deposits, Western Australia—Implications for supergene ore formation and exploration in deeply weathered terrains, *in* Grimsey, E.J., and Neuss, Ian, eds., Nickel '96—Mineral to market, Kalgoorlie, Western Australia, November 27–29, 1996, Proceedings: Australasian Institute of Mining and Metallurgy, Publication Series No. 6/96, p. 185–190.

Brindley, G.W., and de Souza, J.V., 1975a, A golden-colored, ferri-nickel chloritic mineral from Morro do Níquel, Minas Gerais, Brazil: Clays and Clay Minerals, v. 23, p. 11–15.

Brindley, G.W., and de Souza, J.V., 1975b, Nickel-containing montmorillonites and chlorites from Brazil, with remarks on schuchardtite: Mineralogical Magazine, v. 40, p. 141–152.

Bruce, Michael, Niu, Yaoling, Harbourt, Terrence, and Holcombe, Rodney, 1998, Geochemistry and geochronology of the Marlborough ophiolite—Implications for the tectonic history of the northern New England Fold Belt: Geological Society of Australia Abstracts, v. 49, p. 58.

Buchanan, Francis, 1807, A journey from Madras through the countries of Mysore, Canara, and Malabar, v. 2: London, East India Company, 590 p. (Reprinted 2004, [Chestnut Hill, Mass.], Adamant Media Corporation, Elibron Classics.)

Burger, P.A., 1996, Origins and characteristics of laterite nickel deposits, *in* Grimsey, E.J., and Neuss, Ian, eds., Nickel '96—Mineral to market, Kalgoorlie, Western Australia, November 27–29, 1996, Proceedings: Australasian Institute of Mining and Metallurgy, Publication Series No. 6/96, p. 179–183.

Buss, H.L., and White, A.F., 2012, Weathering processes in the Icacos and Mameyes watersheds in eastern Puerto Rico, *in* Murphy, S.F., and Stallard, R.F., eds., Water quality and landscape processes of four watersheds in eastern Puerto Rico: U.S. Geological Survey Professional Paper 1789, p. 249–262.

Butt, C.R.M., 2009, Geochemical dispersion, process and exploration models, *in* Butt, C.R.M., Cornelius, M., Scott, K.M., and Robertson, I.D.M., eds., Regolith expression of Australian ore systems—A compilation of geochemical case histories and conceptual models: CRC Landscape Environments and Mineral Exploration Monograph, p. 81–106, accessed January 25, 2013, at *http://crcleme.org.au/Pubs/Monographs/RegExpOre.html.*

Butt, C.R.M., Williams, P.A., Gray, D.J., Robertson, I.D.M., Schorin, K.H., Churchward, H.M., McAndrew, J., Barnes, S.J., and Tenhaeff, M.F.J., 1992, Geochemical exploration for platinum group elements in weathered terrain—Final report: CSIRO Division of Exploration Geoscience Restricted Report 332R, 413 p. (Reissued as Open File Report 85, CRC LEME, Perth, 2001.)

Butt, C.R.M., and Zeegers, Hubert, 1992a, Climate, geomorphological environment and geochemistry dispersion models, *in* Butt, C.R.M., and Zeegers, Hubert, eds., Regolith exploration geochemistry in tropical and subtropical terrains, v. 4 *of* Handbook of exploration geochemistry: Amsterdam, Elsevier, p. 3–24.

Butt, C.R.M., and Zeegers, Hubert, 1992b, Dissected terrains and tropical mountains, *in* Butt, C.R.M., and Zeegers, Hubert, eds., Regolith exploration geochemistry in tropical and subtropical terrains, v. 4 *of* Handbook of exploration geochemistry: Amsterdam, Elsevier, p. 393–417.

Camuti, K.S., and Riel, R.S., 1996, Mineralogy of the Murrin Murrin nickel laterites, *in* Grimsey, E.J., and Neuss, Ian, eds., Nickel '96—Mineral to market, Kalgoorlie, Western Australia, November 27–29, 1996, Proceedings: Australasian Institute of Mining and Metallurgy, Publication Series No. 6/96, p. 209–210.

Chace, F.M., Cumberlidge, J.T., Cameron, W.L., and Van Nort, S.D., 1969, Applied geology at the Nickel Mountain Mine, Riddle, Oregon: Economic Geology, v. 64, p. 1–16.

Colin, F., Nahon, D., Trescases, J.J., and Melfi, A.J., 1990, Lateritic weathering of pyroxenites at Niquelandia, Goias, Brazil—The supergene behavior of nickel: Economic Geology, v. 85, p. 1010–1023.

Cornelius, Matthias, Smith, R.E., and Cox, A.J., 2001, Laterite geochemistry for regional exploration surveys—A review, and sampling strategies: Geochemistry—Exploration, Environment, Analysis, v. 1, no. 3, p. 211–220. (Also available at *http://dx.doi.org/10.1144/geochem.1.3.211.*)

Cox, D.P., and Singer, D.A., 1986, Mineral deposit models: U.S. Geological Survey Bulletin 1693, 379 p.

Cumberlidge, J.T., and Chace, F.M., 1968, Geology of the Nickel Mountain Mine, Riddle, Oregon, *in* Ridge, J.D., ed., Ore deposits of the United States, 1933–1967 (Graton-Sales Volume): New York, American Institute of Mining, Metallurgical and Petroleum Engineers, v. 2, p. 1650–1672.

Dalvi, A.D., Bacon, W.G., and Osborne, R.C., 2004, The past and the future of nickel laterites, *in* PDAC 2004 International Conference Trade Show and Investors Exchange, Toronto, Canada, March 7–10, 2004, Proceedings: Toronto, Canada, Prospectors and Developers Association of Canada, 27 p.

Data Metallogenica, 2008, The global encyclopedia of ore deposits: AMIRA International, accessed January 25, 2013, at *http://www.datametallogenica.com/index.htm.*

den Hoed, Paul, 2000, An anatomy of furnace refractory erosion—Evidence from a pilot-scale facility, *in* 58th Electric Furnace Conference, Orlando, Fla., November 13, 2000, Proceedings: Warrendale, Pa., Iron and Steel Society, p. 361–378.

Derkmann, K., and Jung, R., 1986, Assessing the potential of Burundi's nickel laterites: Engineering and Mining Journal, v. 187, p. 8–9.

de Vletter, D.R., 1955, How Cuban nickel ore was formed—A lesson in laterite genesis: Engineering and Mining Journal, v. 156, p. 84–87.

de Vletter, D.R., 1978, Criteria and problems in estimating the global laterite nickel resources: Mathematical Geology, v. 10, no. 5, p. 533–542. (Also available at *http://dx.doi.org/10.1007/BF02461983.*)

De Waal, S.A., 1971, South African nickeliferous serpentinites: Minerals Science Engineering, v. 3, p. 32–45.

Dhakate, Ratnakar, and Singh, V.S., 2008, Heavy metal contamination in groundwater due to mining activities in Sukinda valley, Orissa—A case study: Journal of Geography and Regional Planning, v. 1, no. 4, p. 58–67.

Dickson, B.L., and Scott, K.M., 1997, Interpretation of aerial gamma-ray surveys—Adding the geochemical factors: AGSO Journal of Australian Geology and Geophysics, v. 17, no. 2, p. 187–200.

Dill, H.G., 2010, The "chessboard" classification scheme of mineral deposits—Mineralogy and geology from aluminum to zirconium: Earth Science Reviews, v. 100, no. 1, p. 1–420.

Direct Nickel, 2010, The DNi process: Sydney, Australia, accessed August 25, 2011, at *http://www.directnickel.com/process/index.htm.*

Eckstrand, O.R., Yakubchuk, A., Good, D.J., and Gall, Q., compilers., 2008, World Ni-PGE-Cr deposits, *in* World Minerals Geoscience Database Projects: Geological Survey of Canada Beta Release 3.5, accessed August 25, 2011, at *http://apps1.gdr.nrcan.gc.ca/gsc_minerals/gquerycache/nipgecr/DP/dp249.html.*

Economou-Eliopoulos, M., 2003, Apatite and Mn, Zn, Co-enriched chromite in Ni-laterites of northern Greece and their genetic significance: Journal of Geochemical Exploration, v. 80, p. 41–54.

Elias, M., 2001, Global laterite resources: Australian Journal of Mining, v. 16, no. 174, p. 64–65.

Elias, M., 2002, Nickel laterite deposits—Geological overview, resources and exploration, *in* Cooke, D., and Pongratz, J., eds., Giant ore deposits—Characteristics, genesis, and exploration: Hobart, University of Tasmania, CODES Special Publication 4, p. 205–220.

Elias, M., 2006, Laterite nickel mineralization of the Yilgarn craton: Society of Economic Geologist Special Publication 13, p. 195–210.

Eliopoulos, D.G., and Economou-Eliopoulos, M., 2000, Geochemical and mineralogical characteristics of Fe-Ni- and bauxitic-laterite deposits of Greece: Ore Geology Reviews, v. 16, no. 1–2, p. 41–58. (Also available at *http://dx.doi. org/10.1016/S0169-1368(00)00003-2.*)

Evans, D.J.I., Shoemaker, R.S., and Veltman, H., eds., 1979, International laterite symposium: Society of Mining Engineers and the American Institute of Mining, Metallurgical, and Petroleum Engineers, 688 p.

Ferguson, B.A., Camposano, G., and Aponte, J., 1979, Falconbridge Dominicana, ore handling and preparation, *in* Evans, D.J.I., Shoemaker, R.S., and Veltman, H., eds., International Laterite Symposium: New York, Society of Mining Engineers and the American Institute of Mining, Metallurgical, and Petroleum Engineers, p. 152–168.

Foose, M.P., 1992, Nickel-mineralogy and chemical composition of some nickel-bearing laterites in southern Oregon and northern California, chap. E *of* DeYoung, J.H., Jr., and Hammarstrom, J.M., eds., Contributions to commodity geology research: U.S. Geological Survey Bulletin 1877, p. E1–E24.

Ford, K., Keating, P., and Thomas, M.D., 2008, Overview of geophysical signatures associated with Canadian ore deposits, *in* Goodfellow, W.D., ed., A synthesis of major deposit-types, district metallogeny, and exploration methods: Geological Association of Canada, Mineral Deposits Division, Special Publication No. 5, p. 939–970.

Francké, J.C., and Nobes, D.C., 2000, A preliminary evaluation of GPR for nickel laterite exploration, *in* Noon, D.A., Stickley, G.F., and Longstaff, D., eds., GPR2000, Proceedings of the 8th International Conference on Ground Penetrating Radar, Gold Coast, Australia, May 22–25, 2000: International Society Advancing an Interdisciplinary Approach to the Science and Application of Light (SPIE), v. 4084, p. 7–12.

Freyssinet, P., Butt, C.R.M., Morris, R.C., and Piantone, P., 2005, Ore-forming processes related to lateritic weathering: Economic Geology, 100th Anniversary Volume, p. 681–722.

Gac, J.Y., 1979, Geochimie du bassin du lac Tchad. Bilan de l'alteration, de l'erosion et de la sedimentation: Paris, Ph.D. dissertation, ORSTOM, no. 123, 251 p.

Gallardo, Tamara, Tauler, Esperança, Proenza, J.A., Lewis, J.F., Galí, Salvador, Labrador, Manuel, Longo, Francisco, and Bloise, Giovanni, 2010, Geology, mineralogy and geochemistry of the Loma Ortega Ni laterite deposit, Dominican Republic: Revista de la Sociedad Española de Mineralogía, Macla, no. 13, p. 89–90.

Gaudin, A., Decarreau, A., Noack, Y., and Grauby, O., 2005, Clay mineralogy of the nickel laterite ore developed from serpentinised peridotites at Murrin Murrin, Western Australia: Australian Journal of Earth Sciences, v. 52, no. 2, p. 231–241. (Also available at *http://dx.doi. org/10.1080/08120090500139406.*)

Glaskovsky, A.A., Gorbunov, G.I., and Sysoev, F.A., 1977, Deposits of nickel, *in* Smirnov, V.I., ed., Ore deposits of the U.S.S.R., v. 2: London, Pitman, p. 3–79.

Gleeson, S.A., Butt, C.R.M., and Elias, M., 2003, Nickel laterites—A review: Society of Economic Geologists Newsletter, v. 54, p. 9–16.

Golightly, J.P., 1979a, Geology of the Soroako nickeliferous laterite deposits, *in* Evans, D.J.I., Shoemaker, R.S., and Veltman, H., eds., International laterite symposium: New York, Society of Mining Engineers, p. 38–56.

Golightly, J.P., 1979b, Nickeliferous laterites—A general description, *in* Evans, D.J.I., Shoemaker, R.S., and Veltman, H., eds., International laterite symposium: New York, Society of Mining Engineers, p. 3–22.

Golightly, J.P., 1981, Nickeliferous laterite deposits: Economic Geology, 75th Anniversary Volume, p. 710–735.

Golightly, J.P., 2010, Progress in understanding the evolution of nickel laterites, *in* Goldfarb, R.J., Marsh, E.E., and Monecke, T., eds., The challenge of finding new mineral resources—Global metallogeny, innovative exploration, and new discoveries: Society of Economic Geologists Special Publication 15, p. 451–485.

Golightly, J.P., Plamondon, Mark, and Srivastava, R.M., 2008, 43-101F1 Technical report on the Moa Occidental and Moa Oriental nickel laterite properties in Cuba: Prepared for Sherritt International Corporation, 102 p., accessed June 25, 2012, at *http://www.sedar.com/GetFile. do?lang=EN&docClass=24&issuerNo=00002460&fil eName=/csfsprod/data88/filings/01240793/00000001/ f%3A%5Crarcher%5C12941-0001%5C2007AIF%5C43- 101report.pdf.*

Goro Nickel, 2008, The Goro plateau—Geology and water management: Goro Nickel Newsletter, no. 8., 6 p.

Grey, D.J., Schorin, K.H., and Butt, C.R.M., 1996, Mineral associations of platinum and palladium in lateritic regolith, Ora Banda Sill, Western Australia: Journal of Geochemical Exploration, v. 57, no. 1–3, p. 245–255. (Also available at *http://dx.doi.org/10.1016/S0375-6742(96)00040-4.*)

Hay, W.W., and Wood, C.N., 1990, Relation of selected mineral deposits to the mass/age distribution of Phanerozoic sediments: Geologische Rundschau, v. 79, no. 2, p. 495–512. (Also available at *http://dx.doi.org/10.1007/BF01830641.*)

Heim, J.A., Vasconcelos, P.M., Shuster, D.L., Farley, K.A., and Broadbent, G., 2006, Dating paleochannel iron ore by (U-Th)/He analysis of supergene goethite, Hamersley province, Australia: Geology, v. 34, no. 3, p. 173–176. (Also available at *http://dx.doi.org/10.1130/G22003.1.*)

Helgren, D.M., and Butzer, K.W., 1977, Paleosols of the southern Cape Coast, South Africa—Implications for laterite definition, genesis, and age: Geographical Review, v. 67, no. 4, p. 430–445

Horton, J., 2008, Integration of disparate data types for resource estimation—A nickel laterite example, *in* PACRIM Congress 2008, Gold Coast, Queensland, November 24–26, 2008, proceedings: Australasian Institute of Mining and Metallurgy, p. 185–191.

Imrie, W.P., and Lane, D.M., eds., 2004, International laterite nickel symposium: The Minerals, Metals and Materials Society, 745 p.

Jubelt, R., 1956, Entstehung und Erscheinungsweise silikatischer Nickellagerstitten: Zeitschrift fur angewandte Geologic, Heft 8/9, p. 339–347.

Laznicka, P., 1985, Phanerozoic environments, associations, and deposits, v. 1 *of* Empirical metallogeny—Depositional environments, lithologic associations, and metallic ores: Elsevier, New York, 1002 p.

Lelong, F., Tardy, Y., Grandin G., Trescases J.J., and Boulange, B., 1976, Pedogenesis, chemical weathering and processes of formation of some supergene ore deposits, *in* Wolf K.H., ed., Supergene and surficial ore deposits—Texture and fabrics, v. 3 *of* Handbook of strata-bound and stratiform ore deposits: Amsterdam, Elsevier, p. 93–133.

Leneuf, F.N, 1959, L'altération des granites calco-alcalins et des granodiorites de Côte d'Ivoire, forestières et les sols qui en sont derives: Paris, Master's thesis, ORSTOM, 210 p.

Leprun, J.C., 1979, Ferruginous crusts of the crystalline region of arid West Africa—Genesis, transformations, degradation: Sciences Géologie, Mémoire, v. 58, 224 p.

Lewis, J.F., Draper, G., Proenza, J.A., Espaillat, J., and Jiménez, J., 2006, Ophiolite-related ultramafic rocks (serpentinites) in the Caribbean Region—A review of their occurrence, composition, origin, emplacement, and Ni-laterite soil formation: Geologica Acta, v. 4, no. 1–2, p. 237–263.

Li, Jian-Wei, and Vasconcelos, Paulo, 2002, Cenozoic continental weathering and its implications for the palaeoclimate—Evidence from $^{40}Ar/^{39}Ar$ geochronology of supergene K-Mn oxides in Mt Tabor, central Queensland, Australia: Earth and Planetary Science Letters, v. 200, no. 1–2, p. 223–239. (Also available at *http://dx.doi.org/10.1016/S0012-821X(02)00594-0.*)

Linchenat, A., and Shirokova, I., 1964, Individual characteristics of nickeliferous iron (laterite) deposits of the northeast part of Cuba (Pinares de Mayari, Nicaro and Moa), *in* International Geological Congress, 24th, Montreal, 1972, Proceedings: International Geological Congress, p. 172–187.

Llorca, S.M., 1993, Metallogeny of supergene cobalt mineralization, New Caledonia: Australian Journal of Earth Sciences, v. 40, no. 4, p. 377–385. (Also available at *http://dx.doi.org/10.1080/08120099308728089.*)

Maksimovic, Z., 1978, Nickel in karstic environment—In bauxites and karstic nickel deposits, *in* Goni, J., ed., Colloque sur la minéralogie, géochimie, géologie des minéraux et minerais nickelifères latéritiques: Bulletin du Bureau de Recherches Géologiques et Minières—Section 2, Géologie Appliquée, Chronique des Mines, no. 3, p. 173–183.

Maynard, J.B., 1983, Geochemistry of sedimentary ore deposits: New York, Springer-Verlag, 305 p.

Minara Resources Limited, 2010, Minara Resources Limited 2010 annual report: Perth, Western Australia, accessed June 25, 2012, at *http://www.minara.com.au/files/docs/328_2010_Annual_Report_to_shareholders.pdf.*

Monti, R., and Fazakerley, V.W., 1996, The Murrin Murrin nickel cobalt project, *in* Grimsey, E.J., and Neuss, Ian, eds., Nickel '96—Mineral to market, Kalgoorlie, Western Australia, November 27–29, 1996, Proceedings: Australasian Institute of Mining and Metallurgy Special Publication No. 6/96, p. 191–195.

Mosselmans, J.F.W., Quinn, P.D., Roque-Rosell, J., Atkinson, K.D., Dent, A.J., Cavill, S.I., Hodson, M.E., Droop, G.T.R., Pattrick, R.A.D., and Pearce, C.I., 2008, The first environmental science experiments on the new microfocus spectroscopy beamline at Diamond [slide presentation], *in* Geochemistry of the Earth's Surface 8, London, August 18–22, 2008, Proceedings: Mineralogical Society of Great Britain and Ireland, the International Association of Geochemistry and Cosmochemistry (IAGC).

Mposkos, E., 1981, The Ni-Fe laterite ores of Almopia zone: UNESCO International Symposium on Metallogeny of Mafic Ultramafic Complexes, v. 1, p. 317–337.

Mu, W., Zhai, Y., and Liu, Y., 2010, Leaching of magnesium from desiliconization slag of nickel laterite ores by carbonation process: Transaction of Nonferrous Metals Society of China, v. 20, p. s87–s91.

Mudd, G.M., 2009, Nickel sulfide versus laterite—The hard sustainability challenge remains, *in* 48th Annual Conference of Metallurgists, August 23–26, 2009, Sudbury, Ontario, Canada, Proceedings: Canadian Metallurgical Society, 10p.

Mudd, G.M., 2010, Global trends and environmental issues in nickel mining—Sulfides versus laterites: Ore Geology Reviews, v. 38, no. 1–2, p. 9–26.

Nahon, D.B., 1986, Evolution of iron crusts in tropical landscapes, *in* Colman, S.M., and Dethier, D.P., eds., Rates of chemical weathering of rocks and minerals: Orlando, Fla., Academic Press, Inc., p. 169–191.

Nahon, D.B., and Tardy, Y., 1992, The ferruginous laterite, *in* Butt, C.R.M., and Zeegers, Hubert, eds., Regolith exploration geochemistry in tropical and subtropical terrains, v. 4 *of* Handbook of exploration geochemistry: Amsterdam, Elsevier, p. 41–55.

Nahon, D.B., Paquet, Helene, and Delvigne, Jean, 1982, Lateritic weathering of ultramafic rocks and the concentration of nickel in the western Ivory Coast: Economic Geology, v. 77, no. 5, p. 1159–1175. (Also available at *http://dx.doi.org/10.2113/gsecongeo.77.5.1159*.)

Naldrett, A.J., 2011, Fundamentals of magmatic sulfide deposits, *in* Li, C., and Ripley, M., eds., Magmatic Ni-Cu and PGE deposits—Geology, geochemistry, and genesis: Reviews in Economic Geology, v. 17, p. 1–50.

Norton, S.A., 1973, Laterite and bauxite formation: Economic Geology, v. 68, p. 353–361.

Ogura, Y., 1986, Mineralogical studies on the profiles of nickeliferous laterite deposits in the Southwestern Pacific Area: Geological Survey of India Memoir 120, p. VI-1–VI-12.

Ohmoto, H., Watanabe, Y., Allwood, A., Burch, I.W., Knauth, L.P., Yamaguchi, K.E., Johnson, I., and Altinok, E., 2007, Formation of probable lateritic soils approximately 3.43 Ga in the Pilbara Craton, Western Australia [abs]: Geochimica et Cosmochimica Acta, v. 71, no. 15S, p. A733.

Orloff, O., 1968, Etude géologique at géomorphologique des massifs d'ultrabasites compris entre Houailou et Canala, Nouvelle Calédonie: Montpellier, Université de Montpellier, Master's thesis, 189 p.

Panagiotou, G.N., and Michalakopoulos, T.N., 2000, Mine planning and equipment selection 2000: Taylor and Francis Publishing, 975 p.

Pelletier, B., 1996, Serpentine in nickel silicate ore from New Caledonia, *in* Grimsey, E.J., and Neuss, Ian, eds., Nickel '96—Mineral to market, Kalgoorlie, Western Australia, November 27–29, 1996, Proceedings: The Australasian Institute of Mining and Metallurgy, Publication series No. 6/69, p. 197–205.

Peric, M., 1981, Exploration of Burundi nickeliferous laterites by electrical methods: Geophysical Prospecting, v. 29, p. 274–287.

Platina Resources Limited, 2011, Fifield, NSW: Varsity Lakes, Queensland, Australia, Platina Resources Limited, 2 p., accessed March 30, 2012, at *http://www.platinaresources.com.au/files/projects/PC00316_Platina_Factsheet_FIFIELD_LR.pdf*.

Proenza, J.A., Lewis, J.F., Galí, Salvador., Tauler, Esperanza, Labrador, Manuel, Melgarejo, J.C., Longo, Francisco, and Bloise, Giovanni, 2008, Garnierite mineralization from Falcondo Ni-laterite deposit (Dominican Republic): Macla, Revista de la Sociedad Española de Mineralogía, no. 9, p. 197–198.

Proenza, J.A., Tauler, E., Melgarejo, J.C., Gali, S., Labrador, M., Marrero, N., Perez-Nelo, N., Rojas-Puron, A.L., and Blanco-Moreno, J.A., 2007, Mineralogy of oxide and hydrous silicate Ni-laterite profiles in Moa Bay area, northeast Cuba, *in* Andrew, C.J., and others, eds., Mineral exploration and research—Digging deeper, Ninth Biennial Meeting of the Society for Geology Applied to Mineral Deposits, Dublin, Ireland, August 20–23, 2007, Proceedings: Irish Association of Economic Geology, p. 1389–1392.

Rao, A.V., Dhakate, R.R., Singh, V.S., and Jain, S.C., 2003, Geophysical and hydrogeological investigations to delineate aquifer geometry at Kaliapani, Sukinda, Orissa: National Geophysical Research Institute (NGRI) Technical Report No. GW-367, p. 1–40.

Retallack, G.J., 2010, Lateritization and bauxitization events: Economic Geology, v. 105, p. 655–667.

Roqué, Josep, Proenza, J.A., Mosselmans, Fred, Atkinson, Kirk, Quinn, Paul, Labrador, Manuel, and Galí, Salvador, 2008, Preliminary studies on Ni in laterite deposits from Moa Bay (Cuba) by means of µXRF and µXAS using synchrotron radiation: Macla, v. 9, p. 219–220.

Roqué-Rosell, J., Mosselmans, J.F.W., Proenza, J.A., Labrador, M., Galí, S., Atkinson, K.D., and Quinn, P.D., 2010, Sorption of Ni by "lithiophorite–asbolane" intermediates in Moa Bay lateritic deposits, eastern Cuba: Chemical Geology, v. 275, no. 1–2, p. 9–18.

Ross, C.S., Shannon, E.V., and Gonyer, F.A., 1928, The origin of nickel silicates at Webster, North Carolina: Economic Geology, v. 23, p. 528–552.

Royer, D.L., Berner, R.A., Montañez, I.P., Tabor, N.J., and Beerling, D.J., 2004, CO_2 as a primary driver of Phanerozoic climate: GSA Today, v. 14, no. 3, p. 4–10. (Also available at *http://dx.doi.org/10.1130/1052-5173(2004)014<4:CAAPDO>2.0.CO;2*.)

Rutherford, J., Munday, T., Meyers, J., and Cooper, M., 2001, Relationship between regolith materials, petrophysical properties, hydrogeology and mineralisation at the Cawse Ni laterite deposits, Western Australia—Implications for exploring with airborne EM: Exploration Geophysics, v. 32, no. 4, p. 160–170. (Also available at *http://dx.doi.org/10.1071/EG01160*.)

Rye, R., and Holland, H.D., 1998, Paleosols and the evolution of atmospheric oxygen—A critical review: American Journal of Science, v. 298, no. 8, p. 621–672.

Samama, J.C., 1986, Ore fields and continental weathering: New York, Van Nostrand Reinhold Co., 326 p.

Schellmann, W., 1971, Über Beziehungen lateritischer Eisen-, Nickel-, Aluminium- und Manganerze zu ihren Ausgangsgesteinen: Mineralium Deposita, v. 6, no. 4, p. 275–291. (Also available at *http://dx.doi.org/10.1007/BF00201886.*)

Schellmann, W., 1986, A new definition of laterite: Geological Survey of India Memoir 120, p. 1–7.

Schulz, K.J., Chandler, V.W., Nicholson, S.W., Piatak, Nadine, Seal, R.R., II, Woodruff, L.G., and Zientek, M.L., 2010, Magmatic sulfide-rich nickel-copper deposits related to picrite and (or) tholeiitic basalt dike-sill complexes—A preliminary deposit model: U.S. Geological Survey Open-File Report 2010–1179, 25 p. (Available at *http://pubs.usgs.gov/of/2010/1179/*).

Sheldon, N.D., 2006, Precambrian paleosols and atmospheric CO_2 levels: Precambrian Research, v. 147, no. 1–2, p. 148–155. (Also available at *http://dx.doi.org/10.1016/j.precamres.2006.02.004.*)

Shuster, D.L., Vasconcelos, P.M., Heim, J.A., and Farley, K.A., 2005, Weathering geochronology by (U-Th)/He dating of goethite: Geochimica et Cosmochimica Acta, v. 69, no. 3, p. 659–673. (Also available at *http://dx.doi.org/10.1016/j.gca.2004.07.028.*)

Sícoli Seoane, J.C., Castro, N.A., Osako, L.S., and Baars, F.J., 2009, Multispectral imagery applied to nickel laterite exploration—The Conceição do Araguaia discovery, *in* Bedell, R.L., Crosta, A.P., and Grunsky, E., eds., Remote sensing and spectral geology: Reviews in Economic Geology, v. 16, p. 109–122.

Steemson, M.L., and Smith, M.E., 2009, The development of nickel laterite heap leach projects, *in* ALTA 2009 Nickel/Cobalt Conference, Perth, Australia, May 2009, Proceedings: ALTA Metallurgical Services, 22 p., accessed October 17, 2011, at *http://www.ausenco.com/icms_docs/64024_The_Development_of_Nickel_Laterite_Heap_Leach_Projects.pdf.*

Talovina, L.V., Lazarenkov, V.G., and Ugolkov, V.L., 2007, Modern experimental study of supergene and hydrothermal part of polyphase "garnierite" considering increasing of nickel reserves in the Uralian supergene provinces: Freiberger Forschungshefte, C 516, p. 6–9.

Tardy, Yves, 1969, Géochimie des alterations—Etude des arénes et des eaux des massifs cristallins d'Europe et d'Afrique: Mémoires du Sérvice de la Carte Géologique d'Alsace et de Lorraine, v.31, 199 p.

Thiry, M., Schmitt, J.-M., and Simon-Coinçon, R., 1999, Problems, progress and future research concerning palaeoweathering and palaeosurfaces, *in* Thiry, M., and Simon-Coinçon, R., eds., Palaeoweathering, palaeosurfaces and related continental deposits: Oxford, U.K., Blackwell Publishing Ltd., International Association of Sedimentologists, Special Publication 27, p. 3–17. (Also available at *http://dx.doi.org/10.1002/9781444304190.ch.*)

Trescases, J.J., 1973, L'évolution géochimique supergene des roches ultrabasiques en zone tropicale—Formation des gisements nickéliféres de Nouvelle-Calédonie: Strasbourg, University of Strasbourg, Master's thesis, Mémoires Office de la recherche scientifique et technique outre-mer (OSTROM), volume 78, 259 p.

Trescases, J.J., 1975, L'évolution géochimique supergène des roches ultrabasiques en zones tropicale: Mémoire ORSTOM, no. 78, 259 p.

Trescases, J-J., Melfi, A.J., and Oliviera, S.M.B.De., 1979, Nickeliferous laterite of Brazil, *in* Lateritisation processes—Proceedings of the international seminar on lateritisation processes, Trivanfrum, India, December 11–14, 1979: New Delhi, Oxford and IBH, p. 170–184.

Troly, G., Esterle, M., Pelletier, B.G., and Reiball, W., 1979, Nickel deposits in New Caledonia, some factors influencing their formation, *in* Evans, D.J.I., Shoemaker, R.S., and Veltman, H., eds., International Laterite Symposium: New York, Society of Mining Engineers, p. 85–119.

U.S. Geological Survey, 2011, Riddle—Mg hydrous silicate Ni-Co laterite deposit in Oregon, United States of America: U.S. Geological Survey, accessed August 25, 2011, at *http://tin.er.usgs.gov/laterite/show-laterite.php?rec_id=119.*

Utigard, T., 1994, An analysis of slag stratification in nickel laterite smelting furnaces due to composition and temperature gradients: Metallurgical and Materials Transactions B, v. 25, no. 4, p. 491–496. (Also available at *http://dx.doi.org/10.1007/BF02650070.*)

Valeton, I., Biermann, M., Reche, R., and Rosenberg, F., 1987, Genesis of nickel laterites and bauxites in Greece during the Jurassic and Cretaceous, and their relation to ultrabasic parent rock: Ore Geology Reviews, v. 2, no. 4, p. 359–404. (Also available at *http://dx.doi.org/10.1016/0169-1368(87)90011-4.*)

Vasconcelos, P.M., Renne, P.R., Brimhall, G.H., and Becker, T.A., 1994, Direct dating of weathering phenomena by $^{40}Ar/^{39}Ar$ and K-Ar analysis of supergene K-Mn oxides: Geochimica et Cosmochimica Acta, v. 58, no. 6, p. 1635–1665. (Also available at *http://dx.doi.org/10.1016/0016-7037(94)90565-7.*)

Villanova-de-Benavent, Cristina, Nieto, Fernando, Proenza, J.A., and Galí, Salvador, 2011, Talc- and serpentine-like "garnierites" from Falcondo Ni-laterite deposit (Dominican Republic)—A HRTEM approach: Macla, Revista de la Sociedad Española de Mineralogía, n. 15, p. 197–198.

Wells, M.A., 2003, Murrin Murrin nickel laterite deposit, WA: CRC Landscape Environment and Mineral Exploration, 3 p.

Wells, M.A., and Butt, C.R.M., 2006, Geology, geochemistry and mineralogy of the Murrin Murrin nickel laterite deposit: CRC Landscape Environment and Mineral Exploration Open File Report 207, 200 p.

Wells, M.A., and Chia, J., 2011, Quantification of Ni laterite mineralogy and composition—A new approach: Australian Journal of Earth Sciences v. 58, no. 7, p. 711–724. (Also available at *http://dx.doi.org/10.1080/08120099.2011.594 088.*)

Wilkinson, B.H., McElroy, B.J., Kesler, S.E., Peters, S.E., and Rothman, E.D., 2009, Global geologic maps are tectonic speedometers—Rates of rock cycling from area-age frequencies: Geological Society of America Bulletin, v. 121, no. 5–6, p. 760–779. (Also available at *http://dx.doi. org/10.1130/B26457.1.*)

Windley, B.F., Razafiniparany, A., Razakamanana, T., and Ackermand, D., 1994, Tectonic framework of the Precambrian of Madagascar and its Gondwana connections—A review and reappraisal: Geologische Rundschau, v.83, no. 3, p. 642–659. (Also available at *http://dx.doi.org/10.1007/ BF00194168.*)

World Health Organization, 1993, Chemical aspects, *in* Recommendations. Guidelines for drinking-water quality, v. 1 (2d ed.): Geneva, World Health Organization, 65 p. (Also available at *http://www.who.int/water_sanitation_health/ dwq/2edvol1c.pdf.*)

Xstrata, 2011, Nickel, *in* Mineral resources and ore reserves: Xstrata, p. 35–37, accessed January 2013 at *http://www. xstratanickel.com/EN/Publications/Ore%20Reserves%20 %20Resources/x_reserves_resources_201112.pdf.*

Zevgolis, E., Zografidis, C., and Halikia, I., 2010, The reducibility of Greek nickeliferous laterites—A review: Mineral Processing and Extractive Metallurgy, no. 1, p. 9–17. (Also available at *http://dx.doi. org/10.1179/174328509X431472.*)